WOMEN
God's Secret Weapon

ED SILVOSO

Regal

A Division of Gospel Light
Ventura, California, U.S.A.

Published by Regal Books
From Gospel Light
Ventura, California, U.S.A.
Printed in the U.S.A.

Regal Books is a ministry of Gospel Light, an evangelical Christian publisher dedicated to serving the local church. We believe God's vision for Gospel Light is to provide church leaders with biblical, user-friendly materials that will help them evangelize, disciple and minister to children, youth and families.

It is our prayer that this Regal book will help you discover biblical truth for your own life and help you meet the needs of others. May God richly bless you.

For a free catalog of resources from Regal Books/Gospel Light, please call your Christian supplier or contact us at 1-800-4-GOSPEL *or* www.regalbooks.com.

Cover and Internal Design by Robert Williams
Edited by Steven Lawson

Library of Congress Cataloging-in-Publication Data
Silvoso, Ed.
      Women: God's secret weapon/Ed Silvoso.
            p. cm.
      Includes bibliographical references.
      ISBN 0-8307-2887-2
      1. Women—Religious aspects—Christianity. I. Title

      BT704.S55 2001
      270'.082—dc21

5   6   7   8   9   10   11   12   13   14   15   /   09   08   07   06   05   04   03

Rights for publishing this book in other languages are contracted by Gospel Light Worldwide, the international nonprofit ministry of Gospel Light. Gospel Light Worldwide also provides publishing and technical assistance to international publishers dedicated to producing Sunday School and Vacation Bible School curricula and books in the languages of the world. For additional information, visit www.gospellightworldwide.org; write to Gospel Light Worldwide, P.O. Box 3875, Ventura, CA 93006; or send an e-mail to info@gospellightworldwide.org.

D E D I C A T I O N

To our six granddaughters,

Vanessa,
Sophia,
Serena,
Isabella,
Melanie and
Mia,

who most likely will be part of the great host of women
who proclaim glad tidings in the final days
(see Ps. 68:11).

CONTENTS

One of Satan's Greatest Fears

The devil knows that when women find out who they really are and how they play a significant role in his downfall, his kingdom will come to an abrupt end. In fact, God threatened Satan with the anger of the woman and her seed, and He announced a rematch in which Satan will be the defeated one.

Twice Refined

It is key to realize that from the beginning of life on Earth women have given God tremendous satisfaction. In fact, when He created Eve, He gave Himself extra points, calling the sixth day "very good." The creation story provides insights about how God used more refined material and a more sophisticated technique to create Eve, making women twice refined.

God's Trusted Partners

Women have not been relegated to posts as mere privates in God's army; indeed, they have been chosen as key players. The biblical record shows that, from Rahab to Mary to Priscilla, God has used women to transform cities, regions and the world.

Music of the Heart

Women awaken in men the most exciting feelings, but also the most painful ones. Why? Because when Adam and Eve experienced sin, in addition to breaking fellowship with God, they also broke fellowship with each other, creating the gender gap. Men and women need to be reconciled so that the image of God can be fully expressed on Earth.

Spiritual Abuse: Killing with a Silencer

As traumatic as sexual abuse is, another kind of abuse is also rampant: spiritual abuse. Such violations usually happen in pious settings and go unchallenged because they seem so right. Through the ages, Satan has used spiritual abuse to keep women down because he knows that when they discover who they are in Christ, his head will finally be shattered by men and women working together.

Bigotry with a Silencer

Jesus came to recover everything that was lost. The first human loss was the dignity of the woman and her position next to man as a suitable helpmate and partner. Before reconciliation can be attained, the largest gap that keeps the genders apart must be identified and faced: bigotry. The truth about how attitudes and stereotypes have infected the Church must be confronted for biases to be overcome.

The Rematch Takes Place

The first confrontation happened in the Garden, when the serpent deceived Eve and she ate the forbidden fruit. Shortly after that, God promised a rematch. When Jesus shed His blood on Calvary, He bruised Satan's head, mortally wounding him. In the last round of the rematch God will use an all-female army to play a decisive role in vanquishing the devil forever.

The Answer to the Question Why

Even after we understand that women are God's secret weapon, it is still easy to stumble over past hurts and bad experiences. This in turn leads to receiving the grace of God in vain and to the deadly consequences of unremitted sin. A defective understanding of grace perpetuates the gender gap and prevents women from moving into God's assigned roles in His kingdom.

Women's Finest Hour

The greatest harvest in history shall be brought in by men and women working side by side, and Jesus' enemies will become a footstool for Him. Here is a radical message about how women will become equipped, enter the battle and march in the victory parade next to men.

INTRODUCTION

One of the most fascinating verses in the Bible is Psalm 68:11 which describes a company of women who proclaim glad tidings. The intriguing part is not women preaching the gospel but the fact that in this particular case they are convened by the Lord to destroy His enemies. They do such a great job that kings and armies flee in total disarray, making it possible for these women to also loot the enemy camp.

The idea of women preaching is polemical in some quarters, but the concept of women preachers defeating evil armies is novel and controversial, to put it mildly. It is hard to picture women in warfare.

However, at the beginning of the Bible, the first expression of spiritual warfare involves a woman and the devil (see Gen. 3:1-7). Apparently it was not meant to be an isolated incident, because immediately after the encounter, God decreed that the woman and her seed would oppose the devil forever (see vv. 14-16).

The role of women in society, especially in the Church, is one that elicits passionate debate, much of it amplified by the breadth of the social and spiritual gap that separates the genders.

In October 1998, I had the privilege to be on the program at the Promise Keepers' Stand in the Gap rally in Washington, D.C. It was a very moving scene to see more than 1 million men gathered at the Mall to renounce sins of the past and to ask power for the future.

Suddenly a small group of very vocal women, apparently members of the National Organization for Women (NOW), descended on the Mall. They removed some of their clothes and shouted at the men, "Let's see how serious you are about religion.

Look! Look here!" While this was going on, the president of NOW, Patricia Ireland, was giving around-the-clock interviews, relentlessly impeaching the motives of the men at the Mall. The contrast painfully illustrates the breadth of the gender gap.

On May 1, 2000, *Time* magazine published an article titled "The Preacher's Daughter," about Ann Graham Lotz, daughter of beloved evangelist Billy Graham. The writer reported that Mrs. Lotz's ministry has been opposed, and in some cases rejected, by those who otherwise wholeheartedly support her father. The *Time* article reported that at a 1988 pastors' conference "many in Lotz' audience turned their chairs around so as not to face a preaching woman."[1] She is quoted as saying: "When people have a problem with women in ministry, they need to take it up with Jesus. He's the one who put us there."[2]

Whether it is a band of female desperados at the Mall in Washington, D.C., or a female preacher with impressive credentials, such as Mrs. Lotz, what women do easily causes passions to rise.

In the secular arena, I have seen feminist women conduct private wars against men and society. Passion, not reason, drives them. Vengeance, not reconciliation, is their motive. These crusaders can always be found by following the trail of wounded people they leave behind.

I have also seen women in the Church deeply disappointed when the call to ministry they feel God has given them is not recognized, especially by men. Some have become religious feminists. Driven by their hurts, they state their case too strongly and end up increasing the societal pool of pain by causing so much more of it.

On the other hand, the world is a much better place thanks to icons such as Mother Teresa. Unfortunately, the feminists dismiss her as irrelevant for not taking up arms with them. They also look down on women who feel comfortable and satisfied to make home and motherhood their highest priorities in life.

There is a spiritual civil war going on. Even though those who fire the guns make up just a minuscule portion of the overall population, the guns are loud and the bullets hurt a lot of innocent bystanders. I have written this book to encourage men and women caught in this spiritual civil war.

My credentials are very straightforward: I love God, I honor men and women, and I want to see the world reached for Christ. I am a student of the Scriptures who is totally committed to the Church.

I was born and grew up in macho Argentina. Since my earliest days I have had close associations with other boys and men. My father was my best friend, my uncles were my mentors and counselors, and my male cousins were my childhood buddies. With my cousins, I built treehouses, rode horses, played soccer, joined the army, went to school and ran corporations. I have always felt comfortable interacting with men.

On the female side, I have a loving mother and one sister (no brothers), and we lived in close proximity to five aunts. In an Italian-Spanish family such as mine, the term "proximity" carries a more intense meaning than in other cultures. When I say we were close, I mean *very* close. This closeness provided me with a privileged window on the female world as I listened to them talk unguardedly and as I watched their behavior and reactions.

For more than 30 years I have been married to a wonderful woman, Ruth. We have four precious daughters and, as of this writing, six granddaughters. Walking side by side with Ruth, I have been able to deepen my understanding of what a woman is. She has led me by the hand through what to me, a typical male, is an intriguing maze. It has been and continues to be a most enriching experience.

Together we have seen our daughters go from being babies to little girls to young ladies to full women. We have watched them take their first steps in life and in the ministry. As parents we always believed that we were to give two things to our children: feet to stand on and wings to fly with. Today they soar so high that quite often they are our counselors of choice. More recently, from the comfortable position awarded by grandparenthood, we are observing six granddaughters take their own first steps. The road they are on, like their mothers' before them, is dotted with challenges and framed by peaks of joy and valleys of pain.

I am fully persuaded that women are extraordinary creatures, that their God-given potential is way beyond anything we have tapped so far. But I am also aware that the road for women is not an easy one. I want my daughters and granddaughters to succeed. I want every woman to do well!

What does God say about women's role and position in society and in the Church? He is the one who created us, male and female. He is the one who commanded us to marry and cleave to each other until we become one.

There are other questions, too. What provision has He made to deal with the hurts and the pains resulting from gender war? What word has He for women who are oppressed and for men who feel confused and frustrated?

As I searched the Scriptures in my quest for answers, I found that God is deeply interested in seeing men and women reconciled, first to Himself and then to each other. Obviously He is neither a feminist nor a bigot. We know that He is both male and female, because He created men and women to reflect that dual self-image (see Gen. 1:27). He is for reconciliation, and He has plans for men and women to minister side by side in an unprecedented worldwide harvest of souls.

God also intends to use women, alongside men, in a surprise attack to crush Satan's head when the moment comes to put everything and everyone under Jesus' feet.

Women are fascinating. Eve's creation crowned the most intense period of divine creativity on planet Earth. The way God went about it reveals that women are twice refined and that such refinement has a lot to do with God's plans for them in the final days.

At any time now, God will give the command and an army of women preachers will do wonders for Him, surprising everyone, especially the devil himself. In the meantime, God continues to restore the genders so that they can be everything He intends them to be. Read on and be encouraged!

Notes
1. David Van Biema, "The Preacher's Daughter: Billy's Other Kid Goes Big Time With a Series of Stadium Revivals," *Time*, May 1, 2000, pp. 56-57.
2. Ibid.

ONE OF SATAN'S GREATEST FEARS

One of Satan's greatest fears has to do with women. As perplexing as this may sound, what women can do to him constantly torments him. The roots of Satan's anxiety go back to the very beginning of life on Earth when he received the ultimate threat of all time as part of a severe divine judgment.

The Threat

The threat, recorded in the opening chapters of the Bible (see Gen. 3:15) was an elaborate one. It was not an idle fulmination, since God made it and He never fails to deliver. He first curses Satan (who is disguised as a serpent) "more than all cattle, and more than every beast of the field" (Gen. 3:14). After relegating him to the bottom of the animal totem pole, God lowers him even further by cutting off his feet. "On your belly shall you go" (v. 14), He declares, downgrading Satan's mobility to crawling. Finally, God ruins his diet, too, proclaiming: "Dust shall you eat all the days of your life" (v. 14).

But God was not done yet! Next, He threatens the devil with the woman by decreeing that her anger will forever be focused on him (see Gen. 3:15). To drive home the point that it is not a sterile fulmination, God announces a rematch. He even reveals the results: The seed of the woman will defeat Satan, who will have his head bruised while inflicting minor damage to the heel doing the bruising (see v. 15).

Obviously, God is speaking about the advent of the Messiah, but the fact that female anger aimed at the devil occupies such an integral part of God's threat must mean that women have a significant role. Otherwise, why would God use it to frame the first messianic prophecy? I submit to you that there is much more here than what the evil one wants us to know.

Satan is a sore loser and a proud one, too. From the moment God uttered this devastating threat, the devil has been working overtime to twist its meaning. This is why so many people, especially women, have the false impression that Satan has singled them out for harm. Nothing can be farther from the truth. It is the devil who has to watch out, since he is the one described with a bruised head. While women walk upright, Satan must always crawl, making his head vulnerable every time they set their feet down. He is the one who should be afraid, not the other way around.

An Army of Women

Women need to discover this truth. The devil knows that God does not lie—what God promises always comes to pass. This is why Satan has spent centuries belittling women and weaving a web of lies into a formidable worldwide network of oppression to hold them down. He knows that when women find out who they really are, his evil kingdom will come to an abrupt end. He cannot afford to have women walking upright. He desperately needs to keep them down.

> # Satan knows that when women find out who they really are, his evil kingdom will come to an abrupt end.

But Satan cannot do this forever. The Scriptures tell us that the day is fast approaching when God will lift women up and release masses of them into ministry. Psalm 68:11 declares that at a strategic time God will give a command, and a company of women who proclaim the good news will defeat His enemies.[1] An all-female army will bring this about and it will be a surprise victory.

Up to the moment of engagement these warring women will have been forced to lie low, hardly noticed, like gray doves on top of dirty sheepfolds (see Ps. 68:13). At the appointed time, God will tell these humbled women to rise up and fight. When they give chase, God will use them to "shatter the head of His enemies, the hairy crown of him who goes on in his guilty deeds" (Ps. 68:21). Psalm 68 describes the culmination of the rematch promised by God in the Garden, and the element of surprise will be key to victory.

Schoolyard Bullies

I can relate to the doves in Psalm 68 from an experience I had in grade school. It was painful and traumatic in the beginning but ended up defining the rest of my life.

Like many Argentineans, I was raised a Roman Catholic. My mother was pious and devout; my father, a well-respected community leader, was an atheist. From their different perspectives, they each drilled into me the need to be exemplary and to excel at everything I did. In that context they also taught me, in no uncertain terms, never to fight with belligerent children. I was not to stoop to their level; rather, I was to be an example of self-restraint. Fighting was an absolute no-no, especially given my folks's high profile.

As an altar boy and very religious person, I had no qualms with the theory. But the practical side was not as easy, especially when it came to gangs and bullies in school. These schoolyard thugs constantly picked on me because they knew that I would not fight back. I was an easy target. To the bullies I looked like a wingless bird in a fox hole.

Life became extremely difficult at school. Everything I did was turned against me. If I got A's in my classes, the bullies touted F's as the "in" thing. A's were for stupid people, they said. When I became the teacher's aide, a coveted privilege, I was derisively branded the teacher's pet. Every time the principal publicly complimented me, I was savagely booed in private. My books were stolen, my notepads were ripped off, and my lunch money was "confiscated" under duress. My *figuritas*, the Argentine equivalent of American baseball cards, were forcibly "traded," except that this trading was a one-way street into a bully's pocket.

Despite the harassment, I never felt crushed by the bullies. Deep down I knew I was capable of holding my ground with any of them if I so chose, but I felt restrained by my parents' strict orders. The fact that I had the highest GPA in the class and was entrusted to carry the ceremonial flag at public ceremonies reinforced the message that I was different. I could see that I should not lower myself to their level, but it was not easy.

The Fight

Things came to a head when my sister began to attend the same school: The bullies tried to take advantage of her. In the past, these thugs had repeatedly taunted me by referring to my father as a jerk and to my mother as a whore. I was able to endure the false smears because my parents never heard them. But when the "tough guys" began to direct their barrage of filth toward my sister, it hit too close to home. She was on campus, next to me *and to them*!

One day, during a school break, the bullies surrounded and taunted me. They shouted out what they planned to do to my sister and called me a spineless coward who would not fight. Everyone in the schoolyard could hear their obscene slurs.

As the bullies closed in on me, ready for the kill, I felt tremendous tension mounting between the restraining orders under which I had operated all along and the danger fast enveloping me. When the tension reached its boiling point, I felt an unexpected release. Something inside of me commanded me to fight. At that moment I knew that I was no longer to hold back. "Fight" was the word. And fight I did!

In a very short succession the three top gang leaders were laid in a pile on the floor. I had not realized I could dodge punches so well or connect so precisely, but I did both. While I was surprised, the bullies were even more surprised. As I turned to the fourth bully, he froze in his tracks, dropped his fists and ran away. I slowly gyrated 360 degrees to face everybody around me. While holding their gaze I asked, "Who wishes to be next?" They averted their eyes, bowed their heads and quickly dissipated. The three out-of-commission bullies quietly got up and left, deflated and embarrassed.

A New Day
I was never bullied again. In fact, that was the day when all of my peers began to respect me. Word spread that I was not to be

> When women charge into battle, their enemy will be defeated in the most unexpected way. Surprise will be the key element.

messed with. My school accomplishments were no longer derided. My opinions counted. I rose from a position of forced humility to one of undisputed leadership. No one expected it to unfold the way it did, not even myself. But it happened, and it changed things forever.

This is the picture we find in Psalm 68. Silver doves that have been forced to lie low on dirty sheepfolds are suddenly deployed into battle. They unexpectedly defeat an enemy who never thought he would be destroyed by those he had abused so much and for so long (see Ps. 68:11-13). This is the culmination of the rematch promised by God in Genesis 3:15. The restraints that have held women back will be removed. They will hear the word "fight," and fight they will. When they charge into battle, their enemy will be defeated in the most unexpected way. Surprise will be the key element.

Surprise as a Strategy

In the movie *The Patriot*, which is a fictional account of events during the American War of Independence, there is a scene toward the end that fully captures how deadly surprise can be in combat. The Americans were facing well-trained and superbly equipped troops under the command of British Major General Lord Charles Cornwallis.

The Colonist army consisted of some regular soldiers, but it was mostly made up of militiamen who were basically untrained farmers carrying hunting rifles. The British commander openly despised the militia because he had seen it fail in combat so many times. His American counterpart felt about the same way but decided to use this apparent weakness to his advantage. He positioned the militia as the point on the battlefield—this meant they would be the first ones to engage the enemy. As Cornwallis took stock of this maneuver he did not feel threatened. He saw the militia troops advancing against his positions but *knew* they would break down under pressure as they had done in the past.

When Cornwallis sent his troops forward, as expected, the militia turned and fled back toward the hill they had just crested. The redcoats charged ahead, confident that they were about to obliterate the Americans. However, as soon as the fleeing militiamen reached the other side of the high point they hit the ground and lay low. The Colonial army, waiting in ambush, fired their muskets at the unprepared redcoats, who were an easy target as they stood atop the hill. Most of them fell, never to rise again. This surprise attack turned the battle around, and the British left the field in defeat.

The Final Battle

I have written this book to bring home the truth that the devil is afraid of women and that God has kept them in reserve for a decisive role in the final battle. Christ, born of a woman, first bruised Satan's head at Calvary, mortally wounding him by descending to Hades and rising again. Next Christ commissioned His disciples to go to the ends of the earth to dismantle Satan's kingdom. They were assured that at the right moment "the God of peace will . . . crush Satan under your feet" (Rom. 16:20).

The culmination to the rematch that began at Calvary is coming, when the devil will have his head crushed and women, by playing a key role, will more than even the score. Satan knows this because he heard God announce it in the Garden. He has worked hard to keep women down, oppressed and humiliated. He has twisted our understanding of the Scriptures so that women will not be released into ministry. But God is using all of this to lure Satan into a false, and eventually lethal, sense of security.

Because of God's threat and the promised female enmity, there are few things the devil fears more than women moving in the power of the Holy Spirit and men working in partnership alongside. It is about time that women realize they are God's secret weapon for the final battle, as I will show in this book. It is also time that men realize that "it is not good for [men] to be alone" (Gen. 2:18). *Deep* intimacy must be restored for men to reclaim their role as protector and for women to be *fully* released to do what God intended from the beginning: to torment the devil with divinely sanctioned anger in order to keep him down, eating the dust of defeat. This is what this book is all about.

Note

1. The *NASB* reflects the original Hebrew usage of the feminine plural participle to refer to "women." The *NIV, KJV, NKJV* and *RSV* use gender-neutral words. The Hebrew in Isaiah 40:9,10 also attests to women proclaiming the good news to Jerusalem, Judah and the ends of the earth.

CHAPTER TWO

TWICE REFINED

The biblical account of the creation of the world is fascinating. How God made everything out of nothing and commanded planets and constellations as well as all kinds of plants and animals into being is awe inspiring. However, the climax was not reached until God created the first woman.

At the end of each creation day, except the second and sixth days, God looked at what He had brought into being and declared,

"It is good" (see Gen. 1:4,18,25). On the second day, He issued no opinion. However, the sixth day undoubtedly gave Him the most joy. After minting Eve, He pronounced it "a *very* good day" (see Gen. 1:31).

God did not indiscriminately rubber stamp each day with the words "It is good." Silence on the second day and the added adjective on the sixth imply that He did a thorough evaluation before giving an opinion. Undoubtedly, the sixth day is the one that gave God the greatest joy.

Extra Points for God

What happened that God, already pleased with His works the previous days, gave Himself extra points? On the sixth day God first created animal life. He made all the beasts of the earth and said, "It is good" (see Gen. 1:25). Then God created man, and after examining Adam, He stated, "It is *not* good for a man to be alone" (see Gen. 2:18, emphasis mine). That statement, "It is not good," does not refer to the creation of man but to the condition of incompleteness in which Adam found himself at that particular moment. Obviously, God was not fully satisfied with what He saw.

Therefore, God went on to create the first woman, Eve, and right after that He declared, "It is *very* good" (see Gen. 1:31). The rating on the sixth day began as *good,* went down to *not good* and closed as *very good.* The reason for such a dramatic swing was the creation of the first woman. Without Eve the day would have ended on a lower note. Instead, her creation raised it to the highest level of divine satisfaction.

We tend to miss this point. Why? Because after reading the statement, "And God saw all that He had made, and behold, it was very good" (Gen. 1:31), we assume that God was referring to everything He had made during the six days of creation. Even though in a general sense this is true, a careful examination of Genesis 1:31 places that remark at the end of the sixth day and in the context of the creation of Eve (see Gen. 1:28-30). This was the only day God changed His rating of the day's work after creating something. This gives us room to believe that Eve, God's most sophisticated creature, is what moved the level of divine pleasure up several notches.

It is of paramount importance to realize that from the very beginning of life on planet Earth women have given God tremendous satisfaction. Women are not an afterthought or a late addition to God's blueprint for the world, nor are they a piece of equipment created for the benefit of the so-called king of creation—man. No! If man is the crown of God's creation, then women embody the jewels on that crown.

To better grasp the monumental importance of Eve's creation, let's take a closer look at the sequence of events leading to it in the biblical narrative.

Adam Names the Animals
When it became evident that man needed a suitable helper, God sent Adam to name all of the animals in the Garden (see Gen. 2:19,20). Whatever he called them became their name. When Adam was finished "there was not found a helper suitable for him" (Gen. 2:20). I cannot help but wonder why this statement comes right after Adam has gone through every animal on Earth. Could it be that as he moved from creature to creature, he pondered if a suitable helpmate might be discovered among them?

I can imagine Adam looking at a giraffe. Shaking his head, he might have muttered something like this: "She is beautiful. Her spotted coat is fine and her neck is wonderful, but I am afraid I will need a ladder to look into her eyes!" Or, while observing an elephant, at first attracted by its statuesque figure, he might have concluded that it was dangerous to live next to so much poundage. He could be crushed to death at a moment's notice!

The Bible does not tell us why Adam was told to name all of the animals right before Eve was created. However, it is not too far-fetched to speculate that God may have wanted Adam to find out firsthand that no other living creature was capable of filling the void he felt. God may have wished to draw home the point that for Adam to have the perfect helpmate, it would require the creation of someone not yet present on Earth.

A Helpmate for Adam

The account in Genesis tells it best:

> God . . . took one of [Adam's] ribs, and . . . the LORD God
> fashioned into a woman the rib which He had taken from
> the man, and brought her to [Adam] (Gen. 2:21,22).

Obviously Adam did not witness the creation of Eve; he was snoozing at the time. After God removed the rib, He apparently set up His workbench someplace else as implied by the statement that God *brought* her to him. Consequently, Adam had no idea what was coming his way.

Miss Universe 4004 B.C.

What was Adam's reaction when he laid eyes on Eve for the first time? Undoubtedly she was the most impeccable woman ever to walk on Earth. There was no sin, therefore its inherent decay had not yet affected the planet, and least of all the just-created Eve. Her skin must have been absolutely unblemished. She had no need to cover imperfections or apply makeup to highlight anything because she was simply—perfect!

Picture Adam groggily coming out of the divine anesthesia. Earlier in the day he had gone through each pair of animals and now, all of a sudden, he sees something absolutely new that God hand delivered to his mailing address in the Garden. What did he feel and what did he say?

Almost Speechless

Since Adam was in charge of naming all living creatures, he gave her a name, "Woman" (Gen. 2:23). After seeing the greatest display of feminine flesh arranged in the most creative pattern by the best designer in the universe, all he managed to call her was "Woman"? It sounds anticlimactic!

Actually, it was not as bad as it sounds. When we put Adam's remarks in a broader context we see that he said much more than just "Woman." In fact, he created a new word to describe that she was everything he was plus *something else*! Eve was so different from all the animals he had just named and so much like himself ("bone of my bones and flesh of my flesh" [Gen. 2:23]). Yet Eve was not identical to Adam and this undeniable fact required a new word be created just to describe her. In essence, this is what he said: "You are everything that I am plus something else that I cannot identify, and that is why I am calling you *Wo*man."

Adam's one-word description is the modern equivalent of "Wow! What can I say? I am overwhelmed and at a total loss for words! This is too much!"

Twice Refined

There was every reason for Adam to be astonished, shocked and overwhelmed, since the level of creativity God employed to make Eve had not been used before. God created Adam by *shaping* or *forming* him out of *dust* (see Gen. 2:7). This is also true of the beasts: "And out of the *ground* the LORD God *formed* every beast of the field and every bird of the sky" (Gen. 2:19, emphasis mine).

However, in Eve's case God employed a different technique and used more sophisticated raw material. Rather than shaping her out of dust, the Lord "fashioned" (Gen. 2:22) her out of flesh and bone taken from Adam. This made Eve twice refined, first by the more refined raw material used, human flesh and bone, as opposed to dust, and then by the fact that rather than shaping

---

Rather than shaping Eve out of dust, the Lord "fashioned" her out of flesh and bone taken from Adam. This made her twice refined!

---

her, as in the case of Adam and the animals, God fashioned her. The difference between fashioning and shaping is as huge as the contrast between a house built by an apprentice carpenter and one built by the best architect. Fashioning reflects a greater level of creativity and a more refined technique. We can confidently say that women are twice refined!

A Great Mystery

This is also why women are such a mystery to men. They are like innumerable galaxies whose existence and depth extend far beyond the most powerful male telescope.

When God created Eve He did more than just put the most beautiful face to the most awesome body, He created a mystery that would be reproduced through the ages. In the short run, men would be perplexed; in the long run, the devil would be devastated.

I pray that every woman reading this book will lift up her eyes and connect with God to see Him smiling.

Ladies, let the warmth of His pleasure touch every leaf in the tree of your soul that has been frosted by the iciness of indifference and incomprehension. Hear the voice of the Holy Spirit penetrate the innermost part of your being as He declares in a solemn and convincing way that when the first woman was created God smiled and gave Himself extra points—something He does every time a woman is born.

Nothing gives the devil more satisfaction than to see this extraordinary expression of divine creativity overlooked, or worse yet, despised. In fact, this is a key component in his strategy to keep women down. It is a crafty system of lies that Satan carefully maintains to drive home his fabrication that women are an accessory to things but not a key component. Nothing could be farther from the truth!

CHAPTER THREE

GOD'S TRUSTED PARTNERS

Let us picture for a moment a world without women. It would have no preponderance of softness, tenderness, nurture or refined beauty. Men have these qualities, but they project them in smaller dosages; whereas women overflow with them. Without women the world would look like an army base with everything painted white or gray, designed for efficiency at the expense of beauty. As a result of how much would be missing, things that only women are capable of providing with exuberance, an awful sense of incompleteness would permeate the planet.

The Uniqueness of Women

Women are unique in more ways than one. Only they have been entrusted with the ability to host life, to know how it feels to have another human being developing inside of them. The privilege to shelter another life at such an intimate level has been granted exclusively to Eve and her daughters.

> # Women have not been mere privates in God's army; instead, they have been entrusted as key players.

Women are also allowed to nurture a newborn, not just with caresses, which fathers can also provide, but through the most intimate interaction between a female adult and a child: breast-feeding. Visualize a baby being nursed by a loving mother. As you watch her eyes survey the tiny bundle of flesh you will see a picture of total dependency, perfect care and the most sublime transition of nurture from one being to another. Only a woman can paint this picture.

A woman is also the one who predominantly shapes the character of a child during the tender years up to age five. She plants tender gestures in the inner layer of a child's malleable soul during this crucial period. Like a flowerbed with its roots hidden from view, when the child grows older, these seeds will sprout, spreading beauty over the adult landscape in the form of noble deeds. When are the seeds planted? During the nurturing years when a child spends the bulk of his time with a woman: his mother!

At strategic points throughout history, God has used these unique qualities of women. We only have to take a glance at the biblical record to see that God does not consider women second-class citizens. Women have not been mere privates in God's army; instead, they have been entrusted as key players, given pivotal assignments and shared fully in the fruit of victory.

God's Top Commando

Jesus' birth launched the fulfillment of God's threat to the devil. When the time came, God confided the most sensitive secret component of His strategy to redeem humankind—how He planned to introduce the Messiah into the enemy's territory—to a woman, Mary. At a time when compromising such information could have put in jeopardy the divine enterprise, God brought a woman into His confidence.

If anyone thinks Mary deserves no credit, just look at how she fared compared to Zechariah, who received a similar, although not as dramatic, revelation. When the angel announced to each of them that they were going to have miracle babies—Zechariah through a reversal in his wife's barrenness and Mary through the virginal birth—each one asked questions. In response, Zechariah was penalized with muteness while the angel commended Mary. Why? Because Zechariah's inquiries were motivated by unbelief, whereas Mary's reflected a sincere desire to better understand God's message.

Jesus' First Protector

It was a woman who first heard God Incarnate's heart as it developed within her. It was her hands that first touched Jesus' body and wrapped it in swaddling clothes—God's first "woman-made" attire. Think for a moment what this reflects: God Almighty, creator and preserver of the universe, took the form of a baby and became dependent on the care of one of His creatures. When God experienced human flesh, with all its limitations, who was there to meet His needs? A woman. She was Jesus' first teacher, and she became His first disciple. No other person knew Jesus as intimately as she did.

Women's Hall of Fame

The Old and New Testaments are dotted with inspiring testimonies of brave and brilliant women on whose shoulders rested the fate of cities, tribes and nations.

It was Moses' mother, along with his father, who challenged pharaoh's genocidal decree when she preserved the life of the one who would eventually lead millions of Hebrews to freedom. It was another woman, Miriam, who astutely provided a crucial connection to Moses' kinsmen by wisely suggesting that the baby's own mother be his nanny.

Rahab held the keys to the taking of Jericho and by turning them in the right direction she assured the fall of the fortress-city. It was Hannah who cried out to God for Samuel to be born, the greatest prophet and judge Israel ever knew. It was Deborah, an illustrious judge and a proven prophetess, who delivered Israel from the mighty chariots of Jabin, the oppressing king of Canaan and, with the help of another woman, Jael, brought total destruction on him and his leading general, Sisera.

It was Queen Esther who courageously risked her life to save her entire nation, God's people, when it was dangerously threatened by massive genocide.

God himself called Sarah "mother of nations" (Gen. 17:16). Subsequently, she was listed among the heroes of the faith in Hebrews 11.

Priscilla: More Than a Cookie Maker

When Apollos was preaching less than perfect theology, it was Priscilla and Aquila who took him aside to set him straight (see Acts 18:26). This passage does not say that Priscilla baked cookies while Aquila instructed Apollo, but rather that *both* Priscilla and Aquila taught Apollos. This is significant because Apollo was not an amateur preacher; he was "an eloquent man . . . mighty in the Scriptures . . . instructed in the way of the Lord . . . fervent in spirit, [who] was . . . teaching accurately" (Acts 18:24,25) but incompletely the Scriptures.

The fact that Priscilla is listed first when described in a ministry context (see Acts 18:18,26) highlights the prominence of her role and indicates that she was not inferior to Aquila.[1]

A Solid Pillar in the Early Church

One of the main reasons Christianity spread so rapidly in the early years is because its message restored honor and inner worth to half of the world population; that is, women. Romans had such a low view of women that men commonly had recreational sex with other men because women were perceived as inherently inferior. Jewish rabbis completely silenced women when they

were inside the synagogue. Pagans used women as temple prosti-
tutes.

However, Early Church leaders dignified women by teaching
that in Christ "there is neither male nor female; for you are all
one in Christ Jesus" (Gal. 3:28). They acted upon their teaching
by placing women in positions of honor and leadership. Priscilla
was part of the team that founded the church in Ephesus—site
of the greatest power encounter recorded in the book of Acts.
She was there, inside the crux of God's power, when it dethroned
Artemis and brought down the demonic socioeconomic struc-
ture that had controlled Ephesus.

Women are also unapologetically exalted as pillars of the
faith in many of the epistles. Paul identified two women as the
headwaters of Timothy's faith: his mother and his grandmother.
In a letter intended for wide circulation and public reading, Paul
praised nine women as people of faith, courage and proven ministry (see Rom. 16:2-16).

The First Convert
The first European convert was a woman, Lydia, and hers was
the first household to be baptized (see Acts 16:14,15). She was
indeed very assertive in her interaction with the apostles: "*She
urged* us, saying, 'If you have judged me to be faithful to the Lord,
come into my house and stay.' And *she prevailed* upon us" (Acts
16:15, emphasis mine).

Three centuries later, the driving force behind Constantine's
conversion and the subsequent Christianization of the Roman
Empire was another woman, Helena, the emperor's mother.

Jesus' Last Act of Kindness
While most of Jesus' frightened disciples hid at a distance, faithful women stood by the Cross. He hung, naked, not too far from
where the soldiers had cast lots for His robe. He felt forsaken by

His own Father, endured indescribable misery, and yet His last earthly concern was for a woman, His mother. The pain He felt could not obscure the memory that His earthly life began with her taking care of Him. And now, as it was about to end, she stood courageously next to Him, with a pierced heart. In His last act of kindness, he turned her over to the care of His beloved disciple (see John 19:26,27).

Perceiving Spiritual Things

Women have an extraordinary sensitivity to spiritual things. This is why Jesus was able to reveal two of the most powerful truths in the gospels to women. He told Martha that He is the resurrection and the life (see John 11:25-27), and He told the Samaritan woman that He is the living water (see John 4). These women were in a state of confusion when Jesus found them, but both were able to hear, understand and believe profound truths. Think for a moment of the millions of people in the last 2,000 years whose lives have been transformed by these truths!

Ministering to Jesus' Heart

The men watching Mary Magdalene's sublime act of worship accused her of wasting a very valuable flask of perfume. They totally misread her actions when they looked at and judged them through a purely financial, cost-effective grid. Jesus rebuked these men and declared that Mary Magdalene had exhibited great spiritual foresight because she prepared His body for the sepulcher. As He anticipated His imminent betrayal and rejection, Jesus was overwhelmed by sorrow. His heart was taxed with pain; He needed someone to minister to Him. It was a woman who saw the urgency and spent everything of value she had to comfort Him.

Brokenness

Eli accused Hannah of being drunk when, in fact, she was genuinely broken before the Lord. Many times female acts of worship are dismissed as emotional and disruptive. Women are often accused of being too excitable, but this is not necessarily true.

Intrinsically women are not more godly than men are, but they are definitely more spiritual. By this I mean that they have the ability to express a greater range of emotions that enables them to experience worship in a more intense way.

Generosity

God can always count on female generosity when needs emerge in His kingdom. He sent Elijah, in the midst of a terrible famine, to the house of a widow. Elijah asked for everything she had, and she gave it to him! (see 1 Kings 17:13-15).

A group of women used their personal resources to support Jesus' ministry (see Luke 8:3). No man is explicitly identified in the Gospels as a financial supporter of Jesus.

Courage

Women courageously risked their lives on Resurrection morning by visiting the tomb of a convicted criminal whose body was under 24-hour military guard. Also Mary, the mother of Mark, fearlessly hosted a large prayer meeting while Herod was shedding apostolic blood all over town (see Acts 12:12). Likewise, Lydia made her house available to the entire church at a time of violent opposition (see Acts 16:40).

Faith

Women are prone to believe God, with great ease. When God spoke, Deborah had no doubt that God could deliver the Israelites from Sisera's army. Likewise, Mary stood firm in her faith that she could bear a child despite her being a virgin; and the women at the tomb, deep in sorrow, accepted the Resurrection message without hesitation.

After seeing the same empty tomb in the garden that the women had seen, the apostles locked themselves up for fear of the Jews (see John 20:19), and Thomas demanded tangible proof of Jesus' resurrection even though Jesus was standing right there! Most likely Jesus was thinking of the women when He rebuked Thomas, saying, "Blessed are those who have not seen and yet have believed" (John 20:29, *NKJV*).

The Samaritan woman, confused and spiritually unstable after believing that He had the water she needed so badly, was instrumental in evangelizing a city (see John 4:39-42). By appearing first to women on Resurrection Sunday, Jesus made them the first messengers, the first evangelists, the first prophetesses, the first teachers and the first witnesses of His resurrection. This is no small privilege!

Women Play Key Roles

Women have consistently played key roles in God's strategies. They are neither the weaker sex nor an afterthought in God's master plan.

Intrinsically women are not more godly than men are, but they are definitely more spiritual.

Women's bodies are more fragile but definitely not weaker than men's bodies. A china cup is more breakable than a tin cup but also more beautiful. The sturdy drum and the delicate violin are both used to make music. In life, men are the drums and women are the violins. Women are indispensable if the world is going to hear those soft, high notes. They are not a preface, a postscript or an appendix to men. Without women, the story would not be complete. Thanks to the addition of women, we have an even greater book.

Back in the Garden

Let us revisit the moment after the Fall when Eve stood next to Adam and faced God's inquiry. The devil would like women to remember that picture in the most negative light. He wants Eve to be seen as the weak link, the one who brought so much misery to the human race. Even though she was deceived and fell into transgression, let us not miss *an important point*: Eve was the one who identified the enemy! In spite of the shame she felt, Eve understood and described accurately what had happened and who the instigator was, setting the stage for God to announce the rematch. Hers are the only coherent human words spoken.

Let us be strengthened by seeing this passage in Genesis 3 without the distorting lens the enemy has used for so long. Like Eve, women know who the enemy is. Furthermore, Satan knows that *her* seed will eventually destroy him.

It is time for a change. It is time for women not to pay attention to Satan's demeaning remarks, so often channeled through those who look at the exterior and miss the wealth stored inside of them. Women do not need a human platform to be heard because God has given them considerable spiritual height from which to speak. They are designed to be influencers and shapers. Nowhere is this more important than when it comes to playing key roles in God's strategic plans.

Note

1. In Acts 13:2 Barnabas is listed first and Saul (Paul) last among the leaders of the church in Antioch. After they were sent out as missionaries, Barnabas continued to be listed first all through this chapter until verse 42 where Paul's name, for the first time, precedes Barnabas's, and so it remained for the rest of the book of Acts. This reversal in sequence coincides with Paul's taking on a more prominent role in leadership. Also see Ben Witherington III, *Women and the Genesis of Christianity* (London: Cambridge University Press, 1990), p. 220. Witherington writes: "Both she and Aquila instructed Apollos and her name is mentioned first, so that if anyone is indicated by Luke as the primary instructor, it is Priscilla."

CHAPTER FOUR

MUSIC OF THE HEART

Women awaken in men the most intense feelings. Poetry, drama, songs and music capture the depth and intensity of those sentiments in a never-ending harmonious cascade. From the mothers that first held them close to their bosoms to the wives that encircled them with their arms to the daughters they carried on their shoulders, men have had a most intimate relationship with women. Nothing can touch the heart of a man like a woman. She can cause wells of tenderness to spring up all over the rugged surface of his soul.

Castaway in a Sea of Love

I vividly remember the day when, as a teenager, I saw a picture that would change my life.

Soon after becoming a Christian I made a deal with God. I told Him that I did not want to date a series of girls to find out which one I should marry. Instead, I was determined to wait for Him to tell me when the right one came along. It was not easy, but I kept my promise. In the same fashion that the Athenians prayed *to* the unknown god, I prayed *for* the unknown girl God had somewhere for me.

A couple of years later, a friend showed me a picture of a family with several girls in it. All of a sudden I felt the Lord say to me, "The girl in the right lower corner is the one I have for you." I immediately reached for a magnifying glass and told God that He had excellent taste!

As smitten as I was, there was little I could do about it because this girl lived in another province, hundreds of kilometers away, and she attended a church that belonged to a denomination that historically had been antagonistic toward my church's denomination.

Even if she lived in my town or we could communicate at the time, dating among Christians in my native Argentina was a very elaborate process. A potential suitor needed to be invited to visit socially, and this required an advocate. If the girl liked him, permission had to be requested from her parents for courtship to be initiated. If granted, holding hands was as far as things could go until additional clearance was obtained. On strictly a human level, my chances of connecting with her were slim at best.

However, God has a way of bringing about His will. Juan Carlos Ortiz[1] was marrying the sister of the girl in the picture, and they chose to have the civil ceremony in my hometown. The entire family was expected to come. What I did not know was that at about the same time I had heard God's message, that girl had also been shown a picture of our youth group, and she felt God say to her, "The tall guy, in the black leather jacket, he is the one I have for you." When she came to town we were both checking each other out, totally unaware of what the other was doing!

The day she arrived I went to my pastor's house for a "spontaneous" visit, and there was that girl. The moment I looked into her green eyes I became a castaway tossed in an emerald sea. Her hair was a mountain of gold. Her perfect teeth, surrounded by beautiful lips and flanked by dimples, added an incredible frame to a superb picture. Her voice was a purling contralto, and when she picked up the guitar and began to sing, I felt as if I had been transported to heaven.

She touched my heart like nothing else ever had. I knew a river of love existed but was totally unaware of how powerful it was until it invaded my soul. That day my life changed forever. Even though it would take seven years before we held hands at the altar, the day I first saw that girl I was arrested by her. All my emotions became captive to hers. I had set eyes on the sun at noontime, and I was unable to see anyone else. Oases of romance sprang up in my soul. Once again, like innumerable times through the ages since the beginning of the world, a woman had touched and changed a man forever.

That girl, the one I first saw in the photograph, is now my wife, Ruth. Together we have built a love nest where four beautiful daughters, Karina, Marilyn, Evelyn and Jesica, have been born and raised.

The Dark Side of the Moon

While women are capable of stirring the noblest feelings in the male heart, they can also cause the deepest hurts. Music bears witness to that. From the mellow lament of country music ballads to the angry cry of the tango, songs testify to the depth of such ache. Couples who yesterday embraced at the altar, today succumb to alcohol to deaden the pain asphyxiating their once blossoming love. How can something that began so beautifully in a flowerbed end up so tragically in a cemetery plot?

> While women are capable of stirring the noblest feelings in the male heart, they can also cause the deepest hurts.

The root of the problem goes all the way to the beginning of the world. Every sin affects relationships on two levels: vertical, between people and God, and horizontal, between two or more people. When Adam and Eve experienced sin, in addition to breaking fellowship with God, they also broke fellowship with each other. The perfect intimacy they once enjoyed was shattered. The same Adam who days before described Eve as "bone of my bones and flesh of my flesh" and coined the word "woman" to describe her, now disowned her and accused her before God of being the source of his spiritual misery.

The first sin created a gap between man and woman, the gender gap which is the oldest horizontal gap. Since that sad day in the Garden, men and women have suffered its consequences, the most devastating of which is the utter state of incompleteness for both of them when they do not walk in harmony. This in turn has handed the devil a tremendous advantage. Never has the axiom "divide and conquer" rendered higher dividends than when Satan applied it to the gender gap.

Jane Hansen, the president of Aglow International, captured the urgency and the relevance of this when she said, "When God created Adam He made him in His own image, male and female. Both components were in Adam. When God took part of Adam to create Eve, he became totally male while she came to embody the female dimension of God. It is imperative for men and women to be reconciled in order to be able to fully express God's image on earth."[2] Jane Hansen's point cannot be emphasized enough: Men and women *must* be reconciled to reflect God on Earth!

The First Loss

Christ came to seek and save what was lost. On the horizontal level, the first loss was intimacy and equality between male and female. Its consequences stretch through the ages. The need for wholeness between genders goes beyond male and female. It affects institutions, secular and religious, as well as families.

Even though the Old Testament closes on a very high note of hope, predicting that in the last days God will turn the hearts of parents toward their children (see Mal. 4:4-6), for this to happen parents must be reconciled among themselves first. Reconciliation is needed because many, if not most of the problems found among youth today are the visible expression of roots hidden beneath unresolved gender issues which trace their original source back to the Garden.

The Antibody

Reconciliation between men and women is the key. But within this key there is another one: the restoration of women. Men build houses, but women turn them into homes. It is this extraordinary ability to nurse and nurture that has to be affirmed and released.

Like Eve in the Garden, women have been lied to by the devil. Like Adam on that fateful day, men continue to conspire with their silence and judgmental pronouncements. The consequences are painful and have reached epidemic status because every generation is born with this virus.

Even though Christ's death changed everything, most people, even Christians, are still unaware that a divine vaccine is available. Christ injected Himself with the deadly bacteria and overcame it to produce lifesaving antibodies. "For all of you who were baptized into Christ have clothed yourselves with Christ [and] there is neither . . . male nor female, for you are all one in Christ Jesus" (Gal. 3:27,28, *NIV*).

It is about time for the chain of despair to be broken and for women to take the seat of honor that Christ has for them. This is not a passive placement. To the contrary, it is at the forefront of God's plans. God opens the Bible with a threat to Satan, "I will put enmity between you and the woman" (Gen. 3:15) and closes with a picture of a city where multitudes dwell with God forever because *her* seed (Jesus) has crushed Satan's head (see Rev. 21).

The day is fast approaching when women all over the world will hear the word "fight," and fight they will. But for this to happen, men and women need to become aware of the web of subtle lies they have embraced and through which women have been held down.

The power that enforces those lies is the lack of reconciliation between genders. Not only are women incarcerated, but so are men because they will never be everything they are meant to be until they become reconnected to the *suitable help*. Without this reconnection, both men and women are utterly incomplete.

Women are indeed the music of the heart. When they are ignored or abused, it is like the string and brass sections of a symphonic orchestra going mute in the midst of a performance. Worse yet, when women are abused, as we will see in the next chapter, the instruments suffer irreparable damage.

Notes

1. Juan Carlos Ortiz is a well-known Argentine revivalist and author of the best-selling book, *Disciple: A Handbook for New Believers* (Lake Mary, FL: Creation House, 1996).
2. Jane Hansen (presentation at the International Council of Apostles gathering, Dallas, Texas, December 8, 2000).

CHAPTER FIVE

SPIRITUAL ABUSE: KILLING WITH A SILENCER

It was the first evening of a three-day conference for which I was the main speaker. I had prepared with prayer, and when the host pastor introduced me, I was ready to minister. As I approached the pulpit, God entrusted me, in the most unusual way, with very sensitive facts about someone in the congregation.

My eyes were drawn to a lady seated in the front row, someone I had never seen before. She was in her mid-fifties, petite, and had short brown hair. What caught my attention was not her physical appearance but the privileged information God had deposited in my heart about her. He revealed that she was an incest victim and, even worse, that her father was the perpetrator. God also showed me that she had a fragmented personality and had tried to kill people close to her, not once but twice.

As you can imagine, this kind of information is not to be broadcast to the congregation. Consequently, I inquired of the Lord what to do about it, and I sensed Him telling me to wait. For the next two days I ministered from the pulpit, as expected. On the last day, while the pastor and I were having lunch in his study, he said, "Brother Ed, I wonder if you could help us with a most difficult case."

Without hesitating I replied, "Does it involve a lady in her mid-fifties, petite, brown hair?" He assented and I continued, "Has she been the victim of incest, and her father was the perpetrator?" The pastor's mouth dropped in amazement when I concluded, "Does she have a fragmented personality and has she tried to kill people?"

Astonished, he asked, "Who told you that?"

I replied, "God did." The pastor sprang from his chair and went to look for the lady. When she came into the room with the pastor, she told me the saddest story I have ever heard.

Her father had systematically sexually abused her since she was a toddler. Not a week went by that he did not force himself on her, sometimes every day of the week. She told me how when she turned seven she gathered the courage to tell her mother what her father was doing to her. Instead of rescuing her daughter, the mother accused her of making up the story. The mother savagely beat her and, to make things more painful, prohibited her from visiting her grandmother. This was more excruciating than the physical beating because going to her grandma's house was the only respite she had from the sexual abuse. That day she decided to kill herself and headed for a rushing river to jump in. She was saved at the last moment, but the abuse continued.

While in junior high school, this lady had tried to slash her wrists, but was spared again. When she was in her late teens, after her father had raped her, kicked her around on the floor and left the room in anger, she made a vow. She swore that as soon as she had enough money to buy a gun she would kill him, without showing any mercy. Even though she failed to carry out this threat, living in its shadow made life even more miserable.

I could feel the torment inside and around her. Waves of pain surged out of her until they filled the entire room. She went on to tell me that before becoming a Christian she had had five personalities. Following her conversion two of the personalities left, but one of the remaining three was extremely violent, causing her to lose control. Twice she came very close to killing people in her immediate family. The first time she tried to run her husband over with the family car. The second time, while cooking, she almost killed one of her children with a knife.

Locking her pained eyes on me she asked, "Why? Why did this happen to me?" Her gaze reflected the deepest and ugliest well of suffering. She had hit bottom, and now she lay shattered and helpless in a pile of muck.

Sexual Abuse

Sexual abuse such as this woman experienced takes place in a context of blatant violence that makes the hideousness of the act self-evident and undeniable. There is no doubt that Satan brings on such abuse whenever and to whomever he can. It is also clear that God can and will pull sexually abused women out of the muck.

Spiritual Abuse

As traumatic as sexual abuse is, another kind of abuse is also rampant: I call it spiritual abuse. Such violations usually happen in pious settings, often with inspiring music in the background and Bible thumping in the foreground. It looks so right that to denounce it sounds like blasphemy. As a result, it remains largely unchallenged in the Church.

As traumatic as sexual abuse is, another kind of abuse is also rampant: I call it spiritual abuse.

Why are women abused? Why are they violated, not just sexually but also spiritually? Why are so many battered wives told by "spiritual" counselors to blindly submit to abusive husbands—advice that too often has disastrous consequences?

Why are the spiritual gifts that are entrusted to women so often openly disqualified as coming from the flesh or the devil? Some women may not have been abused sexually, but the other kinds of pain inflicted on them may be just as bad because their gifting is impeached by people they have been taught to trust and respect. Repeatedly, women are disqualified solely because of their gender.

Always a Question

Whereas victims of sexual abuse draw immediate sympathy and help, women victimized by spiritual abuse are seen as rebellious, ambitious and non-feminine—they too often are accused of having a Jezebel spirit. The accusations leveled against women are often neatly packaged in Bible verses. It is like being killed by a gun with a silencer. There is hardly a noise but the bullet is definitely lethal.

After 2,000 years of free-flowing grace, why are women in the Church still held back? Why are their voices disallowed except when singing backup for men? Why do they have to constantly prove that God has entrusted them with spiritual gifts? Why do they have to demonstrate that their anointing is as real as men's?

It does not seem to matter whether the person is a young aspiring woman minister in Latin America or Anne Graham Lotz, the daughter of world-famous evangelist Billy Graham, who has inherited her father's mantle for evangelism. It seems that women, no matter who they are or what they try to do in ministry, constantly need to prove their legitimacy. It does not matter that they are godly or that their ministry brings unquestionable glory to God. It too often makes no difference that multitudes are saved and edified through their work.

If the officiating person is a woman, the results are automatically questioned, usually by men. When asked for a reason, often the answer is "She is a woman. She is not supposed to be doing that." It sounds as if a case of AIDS is being discussed: The carrier has to be quarantined and the virus destroyed. All of this constitutes spiritual abuse.

When Women Look Up

Let us not despair: Freedom and healing can be found for people of *both* genders. Ladies, if you feel you have fallen too low to hope anymore, let me remind you that once you hit bottom there is only one way to go—up!

And up you will go with God's help, because time and prophecies are on the side of the restoration of women. When Peter preached his first sermon, outside the Upper Room, he quoted an Old Testament prophet, Joel (see Acts 2:14-21). God had spoken through Joel many years before to announce that in the last days sons and daughters, bond servants and maidservants, male and female, would be restored and would stand together in ministry in the midst of a river of revival.

This river will be so deep and so wide that it will engulf *all flesh* so that "everyone who calls on the name of the Lord will be saved" (Acts 2:21) and ushered into an era of harmony between men and women. Gender reconciliation will be the distinctive mark of the final revival, the mightiest one, since it will sweep the whole Earth and touch all flesh. Men and women will minister side by side in the midst of the most awesome display of God's power. At that precise moment, Satan's head will be crushed forever.

To better understand how this will unfold, we need to see why Satan targeted Eve rather than Adam. We will look closer at this in the next chapter.

CHAPTER SIX

BIGOTRY WITH A SILENCER

It was Eve's remarkableness that made her the target of Satan's scheming. Her strengths rather than her weaknesses singled her out in the devil's mind. Eve, as an expression of God's most sophisticated craftsmanship, especially her unique ability to host and nurture life, must have caught Satan's attention. As such, she was more vulnerable to compounding damage.

Satan set up a trap, Eve fell into it and on that day much was lost. Through God's most exquisite and delicate expression of creativity the door was opened for venom to contaminate the whole creation, which brought pain, degradation and cataclysmic misery to the entire race, which she and Adam founded. The damage was of such great magnitude that to reverse it would require the intervention of God Himself through a miraculous birth many years later.

The first sin, in addition to separating man from God, created the first human gap, the gender gap. Because this separation involves men and women at the most intimate level it also affects everything else in the world. God's image is reflected in both the man and the woman. Of all the things He created, the only ones after His own image were the man and the woman. A gap separating the two tarnished that image. A gap that degrades women makes restoration impossible. A gap that keeps men from seeing women as their partner leaves them in a pitiful state of incompleteness. This gap has to be bridged for the image of God to be fully expressed again on planet Earth.

The Gender Gap

Jesus came to recover everything that was lost, from the very first to the last thing. The first human loss was the dignity of the woman and her position next to man as suitable help and partner. This is how God treated Adam and Eve before the Fall. He blessed and commanded *both* of them to fill and subdue the Earth and gave *both* of them power to rule over all living beings (see Gen. 1:28). As stewards of God's creation, they were equal partners. Such parity was destroyed when sin entered the world (see Gen. 3:16). Consequently it should be the first human loss to be recovered this side of Calvary. Unfortunately this has not been the case.

The Coming Awards Ceremony

When Jesus Christ cried out "It is finished" (John 19:30), the transaction was settled from God's perspective. Sin was dealt with, no longer to constitute a barrier between heaven and Earth. However, as far as life on Earth is concerned, the position held by women before the Fall is yet to be reinstated. God won the prize, but the Church still has to hold the awards ceremony. This is confirmed by the still subservient position of women in the world, even in the Church.

I see evidence of this when I do my seminar on city-reaching. One of the key sessions deals extensively with Paul's exhortations, in the book of Ephesians, to restore every broken relationship in order to be able to confront the forces of evil (see Eph. 6:11). To that effect, Paul commands Christians to bridge six gaps affecting ethnic groups (chapter 2), saints (chapter 3), ministers—apostles, prophets, evangelists and pastor-teachers— (chapter 4), husbands and wives, parents and children (chapter 5) and masters and slaves (chapter 6).

When the participants are exhorted to repent of prejudice, bigotry and racism, a powerful public display of repentance takes place. Charismatics confess sins against non-charismatics. Parents kneel before children and vice-versa. Caucasians and people of color renounce racism. Each one of the gaps is promptly dealt with except one, the gender gap.

Time and again I see men in a pool of tears embracing the feet of others seeking absolution, who suddenly stiffen their backs when told to ask forgiveness of women in the audience. They adopt a defiant posture as if to say, "What do you mean when you say that we need to repent before women?" The fact that the gender gap exists and needs to be bridged eludes them completely.

This reaction becomes even more bellicose when I suggest repentance should also be directed to women in ministry. "Women in ministry?" The thought is handled with the indignation reserved for a blasphemous act. It does not matter that women have been in ministry for ages and that the imprint of their walk with the Lord is all over the Church. The notion that public acknowledgment and repentance might be called for is as disgusting as bringing a dirty family secret out into the open.

The Subtleness of Bigotry

A colleague of mine was critical of a lady minister who had actively participated in acts of reconciliation in one of our conferences. He was also upset when some of us suggested that in dealing with this sensitive and elusive issue it is best to begin by admitting that everyone has some degree of bigotry and work from there. His point was, "We are not bigots. Why make such a fuss of something that is a non-issue? It bothers us (men) when it is insinuated that we are bigots, especially by ladies."

A couple of my associates and I met with him and his team to discuss his concerns. I should say that we constituted a fine group consisting of seasoned ministers, pastors and theologians. We were all "men of the cloth," knowledgeable of the Scriptures and eloquent preachers.

After an opening prayer it was suggested that we examine ourselves for the usual male prejudices against women. Man after man expressed conclusive self-absolving opinions on the matter. After an extensive one-sided discussion, my colleague offered his male associates as character witnesses and with absolute sincerity stated, "I do not believe I have any bigotry in me." Immediately a drizzle of absolution descended on the group. It felt good to hear someone state conclusively that we were not a bunch of bigots!

I looked around and counted 12 men and one woman—she sat in a corner with sealed lips. If the situation had not been so pathetic it would have been comical: Here we were, a group of 12 men discussing women and pompously absolving ourselves of any bigotry! How typical of us men to acquit ourselves on a matter affecting ladies without bothering to ask the only female present to express her perception.

Roots of Bigotry

Bigotry has existed from the very beginning. Adam exhibited it right after the Fall when, in self-defense, he blamed "the woman whom Thou gavest to be with me" (Gen. 3:13). However, very few things have *legitimized* more our biased view of women than the theological reflection developed in the midst of the religious wars at the time of the Reformation, a time when the foundation for our current theology was laid.

Bigotry has existed from the beginning. Adam exhibited it right after the Fall when, in self-defense, he blamed "the woman whom Thou gavest to be with me."

Up to that moment Catholic theology had severely limited women. As far as ministry went, the most women could aspire to was to become a nun, except those who did become martyrs for the faith. This restrictive view of women reflected Middle-Ages thinking rather than the prominence accorded to them in the Scriptures. In such a context any new gender theology was bound to be negatively viewed by the male religious scholars who ran the newly established and still-untested Protestant theological mills.

Satan must have foreseen fiery preachers spreading the good news all over and realized that the entire world was about to slip out of his grasp. He had ruled this world with impunity for nearly a millennium, a time when the Scriptures became inaccessible, when Christianity was unhealthily ritualized and Church leadership was often selected by corrupt secular forces. I suspect that Satan, cognizant that he was powerless to stop the newly discovered message of salvation, instead concentrated his resources on blinding the eyes of the new theologians to the restoration of women. If he could not prevent the whole world from hearing the liberating message, he would at least keep half of it from experiencing freedom at its fullest.

A Bad Model
Satan's best shot was with scholars caught in the fiery passions ignited by the religious wars. A case in point involves a fine and brave Scotsman whose love for his country was second only to his love for God: John Knox.

He was a Protestant reformer and a patriot, and, as such, he would do anything to prevent the throne of his beloved Scotland from going to a Catholic monarch. When Mary, Queen of Scots, claimed it, Knox fought her with everything at his disposal. Being a theologian, theology became his weapon of choice, but he soon found himself torn between opposing issues. On one hand, as a practical expression of the principle that all authority is instituted by God, he believed that God appointed monarchs.

But this conviction clashed with his visceral anti-Catholicism. He could not accept that God would appoint a Catholic to the throne, even though Mary's legitimacy was unimpeachable.

To resolve this tension, he affirmed the principle of authority in general while challenging Mary's right to the throne, mostly on account of her womanhood. As a theologian, he interpreted biblical passages that deal with the role and the position of women in the most restrictive way possible. By overemphasizing what the Scriptures tell women *not* to do, John Knox blinded himself and his followers to the many things to which women are entitled.

A Weak Theology

Knox, who made great contributions to the Church on many matters, was not dishonest in his handling of the Scriptures, but out-of-control political passions sweeping his land tainted his conclusions. In his drive to deny Mary the right and authority to rule, he infringed upon women's authority in general. He did this at a time when Protestantism was emerging as a powerful force in Christendom. By implanting his subjective opinions during the formation of the Protestant church, he unsuspectingly set in motion a process that took these opinions all over the earth as the movement expanded its frontiers. The greatest loss, though, was to miss the opportunity to produce the theological reflection necessary to see women fully restored.

Today, most of those who stiffen their backs when called to humble themselves before women fail to realize that the theological reflection behind their beliefs is relatively young. Its roots go back fewer than 500 years. We need to put into perspective the minuscule pond from which, too often, demeaning gender theology has been drawn. Faulty assumptions about the role and position of women in the Church have caused us to interpret key passages in a restrictive way. One such passage is 1 Timothy 2:8-15:

Therefore I want the men in every place to pray, lifting up holy hands, without wrath and dissension.

Likewise, I want women to adorn themselves with proper clothing, modestly and discreetly, not with braided hair and gold or pearls or costly garments; but rather by means of good works, as befits women making a claim to godliness. Let a woman quietly receive instruction with entire submissiveness. But I do not allow a woman to teach or exercise authority over man, but to remain quiet. For it was Adam who was first created, and then Eve. And it was not Adam who was deceived, but the woman being quite deceived, fell into transgression. But women shall be preserved through the bearing of children if they continue in faith and love and sanctity with self-restraint.

When we study this passage through a traditional grid, we find three restrictions imposed against women:

- they should not adorn themselves excessively (v. 9);
- they should receive instruction quietly, with entire submissiveness (v. 11);
- they should neither teach nor exercise authority over men (v. 12).

The stated reasons are that man was created first (v. 13), and that Eve was deceived and fell into transgression (v. 14).

First Female Dress Code

The context for this passage is Paul's instructions to men *and* women on how to conduct themselves and participate in public prayer meetings (see 1 Tim. 2:1-8). Before we analyze the restrictions, let us make sure we do not miss three very positive points.

1. Women are permitted to participate in public religious meetings (see 1 Tim. 2:9). This is a significant departure from what was customary. At the time, neither Romans nor Jews allowed women to be actively involved in religious ceremonies. Pagan temples employed them as prostitute priestesses, a very debasing occupation.

   The concept of women participating in public meetings was so novel that Paul had to get down to basics: What should women wear? If Paul were not discussing a public meeting, there would be no need to give instructions on how to dress. He further sought to make clear that the wrong attire would not distort the purpose of the meeting. Unbelievers who saw Christian women in public should not be prevented from recognizing their godliness on account of their looks (see 1 Tim. 2:10).

2. Paul specified that women must adorn themselves with good works. Since the text is presenting these works as something that bystanders should be able to notice, it follows that Paul is talking about *public* works. They should be seen as easily as the dresses.

3. He stated that women must now be taught in the same manner and environment in which men have been traditionally taught.

Unfortunately, when we come to Paul's point that women should not teach or take authority, we often see these restrictions as the main point of Paul's teaching. When we do this we miss what he *did* allow them to do. Paul permitted them to participate in religious meetings, to do public good works and to receive teaching. Let us take a closer look at the last point on the list.

A Great Social Revolution

Universal education has made it possible for girls to be taught alongside boys. This is such a well-established right that for us in the twenty-first century, it is impossible to appreciate the revolutionary nature of Paul's remarks in the context of his time. In Paul's day women were not taught. What he introduced was far more radical than the French and the American revolutions combined since it affected half of the world's population. Paul specified that women were no longer to be kept in ignorance but should be instructed in the same manner that men had been through the centuries.

Rather than merely a simple step, this is a giant leap forward for women since in New Testament times women, although considered superior to animals, were seen as inferior to men.

Creation and Sin

Paul, having stated that women are entitled to three extraordinary privileges, moved on to discuss two restrictions: they are not to domineer men nor are they to teach them in a contentious way.[1] To show that this is not an arbitrary decision on his part, he provided a twofold rationale: Adam was created first (v. 13) and Eve was the one who fell into transgression (v. 14). Traditionally we have welded these two points and subsequently drawn the wrong conclusion.

Paul presents two different things. One is the order of creation—Adam was created first. The other is the order in which sin was *introduced*—first through Eve's transgression. These two orders cannot be combined because they are incompatible. The first one represents an absolute that cannot be altered; whereas the second is conditional and as such is subject to modification.

When seen as one, the *immutability* of the order of creation is incorrectly transferred to Paul's restrictions, preventing us from seeing the *relativity* of the consequences of Eve's transgression, which have been voided by the Cross. Separating the two is essential in order to understand what Paul is really teaching about women.

Not to Be Mixed

The order of creation is inalterable and irreversible. Adam was created first, and there is nothing anyone can do to change it. On the other hand, the order in which sin first *entered* the human race is the result of a choice made by someone other than God; in this case, Eve. She chose to disobey God, thus becoming the first one to fall into transgression. It is even possible that after losing her own innocence she knowingly contributed to Adam's fall by inviting him to eat the fruit she already knew was evil.

Harsher Punishment

God passed sentence and punished Adam and Eve with separation, pain and hardship (see Gen. 3:16-19), but to Eve He added a demotion: He made her desire subject to Adam (v. 16). Part of the reason for this is that her transgression constituted a premeditated act and, as such, deserved sterner punishment.

How did this additional penalty play out through the years? Men, exercising this license to rule over women, chose to keep them ignorant and in an inferior social status. This is the direct consequence of Eve's transgression. That is why Paul told men to eliminate it by reversing the state of ignorance imposed on women when their desire was made subject to their husbands. In order to counterbalance the consequences of the first sin, Paul instructs men to bring women up to par by teaching them. This is not a demotion but a promotion!

If Paul was scolding someone it was men, not women. When he connected the need for men to instruct their wives and Eve's transgression, it was to highlight the fact that Eve fell because Adam failed to instruct her. He was the one who received the prohibition to eat from the tree and was cognizant of the details, whereas she had heard it secondhand. Judging by the way Eve mishandled the information when confronted by the serpent, Adam had apparently not given her proper instructions.

Satan questioned Eve in a deceitful manner by including all the trees in God's prohibition. Eve replied that such was not the case but overreacted by adding that the tree should not be touched (see Gen. 3:3). God never said not to touch it, yet in a context of lies managed by Mr. Liar himself, and with Eve handling secondhand information, the truth was twisted. Adam saw that Eve was being misled and also that she was responding incorrectly. Nevertheless, he stood next to her and did nothing to instruct her. Paul's admonition to men is that they should not fail their wives the way Adam failed his.

The First Frame

Paul's restrictions about women not being allowed to teach must be seen as a principle that is in process rather than a fixed rule. He wrote to a specific group of people *in the first century*—to a woman or a group of women who were contentious and domineering, as suggested by the command in 1 Timothy 2:11-12 to be "in full submission" and to show "quietness [a peaceable attitude]." The tenet he introduced is universal and trans-cultural, but the local situation he spoke into was neither. We tend to view Paul's instructions as if they are the final picture, when in reality they are the *first* frame in a movie reel. Paul addressed the demotion of women at its lowest point—at the onset of Christianity—and introduced a principle to restore it to its original splendor. To accomplish this would undoubtedly take time.

From his vantage point, at the beginning of the Christian era, Paul described the first frame on the reel. This frame features untaught women who must be taught in order to conform to the emerging dispensation of grace. As the film rolls into the future a new picture is bound to emerge—as it progresses, the picture of the restoration of women will certainly be more developed than the one in Paul's time.

Learning Comes Before Teaching

Paul admonished women not to teach, primarily because up to that moment they had not been taught, due to the consequences of Eve's transgression. A basic prerequisite for teaching is to have something to teach. Since women had not been taught they were

> Paul admonished women not to teach, primarily because up to that moment they had not been taught.

at a disadvantage when it came to teaching, especially on religious matters. However, after Christ's death, which dealt with Eve's sin, women had to be taught.

How do people acquire something to teach? They must first be taught! The implication is unavoidable: Once women are taught, they should be able to teach.

When we separate the order of creation from the order in which sin was introduced to the human race, rather than treating them as indissoluble parts of a whole, we see the role of women in a light that is far more consistent with the Scriptures and with the distribution of spiritual gifts in the Church.

Paul cannot be disallowing all women in Ephesus from teaching and exercising any kind of authority over men in general, because He certainly knew Priscilla had been one of his coworkers in Ephesus, where Timothy was now overseeing churches, and she, along with her husband, fruitfully taught Apollos (see Acts 18:26).

Furthermore, in 1 Timothy 2:11 Paul is no longer writing about "women" in the plural as he was earlier in 1 Timothy 2:9-10. Here he notes "a woman" in the singular referring to one woman, or to a restricted number of women at Ephesus.[2]

This kind of prohibition against a specific contentious domineering wife, or wives, is a far cry from a blanket prohibition against godly women teaching or exercising the ministry to which God has called them in the Body of Christ.

Salvation Through the Bearing of Children?

"But women shall be saved through the bearing of children if they continue in faith and love and sanctity with self-restraint" (1 Tim. 2:15, NIV).

In this verse Paul states that "women shall be saved through the bearing of children." What kind of salvation is he talking about? It cannot be from eternal damnation because that salvation has been provided by Jesus Himself. According to the context it has to be salvation from the consequences of Eve's transgression (v. 14), since this is the subject under discussion. How can bearing children produce this salvation?

The general interpretation points to the bearing of the child, Jesus, as the seed of the woman. Nevertheless, in a more specific way it may refer to evangelism as inferred by the Greek word used here. The word is *teknogonea*, which in the New American Standard Version is translated as "bearing of children." However, teknogonea, which is used only once in the New Testament, does not just mean *bearing* children but also *begetting* children. Physiologically speaking, women can bear children, but they cannot beget them. Begetting is something only men can do because it entails depositing the seed inside the woman. Therefore, it follows that Paul must be referring to something else. I would like to suggest it is the begetting of spiritual children.

This is consistent with the context of 1 Timothy 1:15–2:15 which is the passage that shows us how to do prayer-based evangelism, or what we now call prayer evangelism. It is also harmonious with the well-known section on women evangelists in Psalm 68:11 where we read, "The Lord gives the command; The women who proclaim the good tidings are a great host."

Women as Evangelists

It is undeniable that women constantly play major roles in leading people to the Lord, as grandmothers, aunts, mothers and wives. Also, some of the most effective public evangelists are women. This is true whether we are looking at door-to-door evangelism in the Third World, or at Kathryn Kuhlman, Aimee Semple McPherson or Mother Teresa, or nowadays at Cindy Jacobs or Anne Graham Lotz. Whether we agree or disagree with their theology or methodology, we cannot deny that these women have led multitudes to Christ.

By using the picture of bearing children, with its connotation of bringing new life into the world, Paul seems to suggest that their effectiveness in ministry will reverse the consequences of Eve's transgression. In other words, let the fruit reveal the true roots of this still uncatalogued tree. There is biblical precedence for this that involves God introducing the radical principle that Gentiles can be saved without first becoming Jews. Just as Peter validated Cornelius's conversion through a verifiable spiritual experience—speaking in tongues (see Acts 11:15-18)—Paul states that as properly taught women begin to minister effectively, their restored status will be recognized when the fruit of such ministry becomes evident. Let us keep in mind that Paul opens this section on women by emphasizing the need for them to do *good works* that provide a tangible side to their inner godliness.

Sin and Iniquity

Paul made the working out of this salvation dependent upon women being able to continue "in faith and love and sanctity with self restraint" (1 Tim. 2:15). Why would Paul make this a condition for women to be free from the consequences of Eve's transgression? It has to do with the crucial difference between sin and iniquity.

Sin can be described as the evil act itself and iniquity as its consequences. Sin is the disobedience proper; iniquity is the mark left on those involved or touched by it. Today the *sin* of slavery is no longer practiced in the United States, but the *iniquity* of slavery—its consequences—is painfully evident. African-Americans struggle under appalling and debasing social, economic and moral conditions. They have alarmingly high rates of teen pregnancy, unemployment and unwed mothers, while they score extremely low on college entrance exams.

God will not hold the sins of the parents over the children after the fourth generation because those sins have been forgiven through the atoning death of Jesus Christ. To revisit them would be like attempting to cash a check twice, especially one that has a red stamp on its face stating: "PAID IN FULL."

On the other hand, iniquities—the consequences of those sins—are still among us because they transcend generations and must be removed. Sin in itself is intangible but its consequences are not. This is where the Church comes in. Once our intangible sins are washed away, we must move on to reverse their tangible consequences, first in our own lives and then in the lives of those touched by such sin and eventually in society itself. This must be done through repentance, restitution and restoration that exemplifies the opposite of what sin did.

Because Jesus' atoning blood symbolizes a divine "PAID IN FULL" on the promissory note Satan held against humankind, he no longer has rights to the property he obtained through deception in the Garden, because Jesus redeemed the note. This is why the Church has been commanded to repossess that which was legally awarded at Calvary. To accomplish this, we must take the next step and remove all existing iniquities by operating in a spirit opposite the spirit of the sin that created them. For example, in the case of slavery, whites are to serve, honor and give rather than to take from their African-American brethren. The key is making restoration in the *opposite* spirit.

Self-Restraint Above All Else

This is something that cuts both ways. On the one hand, men are instructed to reverse centuries of oppression and to teach their wives until they have been brought up to par. On the other hand, the blueprint for women to be saved from the consequences of Eve's transgression is outlined in 1 Timothy 2:15, which instructs women to operate in the opposite spirit of what brought defilement in the first place. They are to continue in faith, love and sanctity with self-restraint in order to develop a lifestyle that reflects the exact opposite of what gave sin entrance in the Garden.

At the moment of the Fall Eve did not believe God. Christian women are to believe (have faith). Eve did not love Adam enough to keep from luring him into eating something evil she had tasted. Christian women are to love their husbands, even those who are disobedient to the Word (see 1 Pet. 3:1). Eve chose to defile herself and to extend such defilement to Adam. Christian women are to remain in sanctity by means of good works, as befits women making a claim to godliness (see 1 Tim. 2:10).

Above everything else, Christian women are to display self-restraint. Why self-restraint? First, because self-restraint is what Eve failed to exercise in the Garden when she chose to act on her own. Second, if Christian women jump the gun on the issue of female restoration they will put in jeopardy God's secret plan for them in the final days, as we will see in the next chapter.

Notes

1. In 1 Timothy 2:11-15 Paul writes, "I am not permitting [Greek present indicative *Ouk epitrepo,* a progressive tense] a woman/wife [Greek *gune*] to teach or to domineer [Greek *authentein*] a man/husband [Greek *aner*]." The Greek verb *authentein* means "to domineer," not simply "to exercise authority," according to the standard Greek English lexicon of the New Testament (Bauer, Arndt, Gingrich, Danker, *A Greek Lexicon of the New Testament* [Chicago: University of Chicago Press, 1979] p. 121).
2. Dr. Gary Greig has enlightened me as to the meaning of the Greek word "gune" in 1 Timothy 2:11-15 which should be translated "wife," not "woman" because Paul refers to Adam and Eve, the first husband and wife. Therefore, 1 Timothy 2:12 should be translated as "I am not permitting a wife to teach or to domineer a husband."

CHAPTER SEVEN

THE REMATCH TAKES PLACE

"And I [God] will put enmity between you and the woman, and between your seed and her seed; He shall bruise [or crush] you on the head and you shall bruise him on the heel" (Gen. 3:15).

When God spoke these words He made it crystal clear that a rematch would take place. A rematch, to be such, has to involve the original contenders. Since God describes the rematch in the context of enmity between the woman and the serpent, it is not entirely far-fetched to think that women would play an integral role.

The seed in Genesis 3:15 is, of course, a legitimate reference to the Messiah who would be born of the woman. Clearly, when Christ shed His blood at Calvary He bruised Satan's head, mortally wounding him. As far as Satan's pre-Calvary position in the heavenly places is concerned, he was dethroned and the lordship of Jesus took permanent hold.

As soon as the Church was established and Jesus' disciples began their evangelistic journey "toward the ends of the earth," Satan's dominion on Earth began to crumble. First, Jerusalem was filled with the doctrine of the apostles (see Acts 5:28), followed by a succession of cities in Judea and Samaria. Soon, Ephesus and the Roman province of Asia were liberated when "all . . . heard the word of the Lord, both Jews and Greeks" (Acts 19:10). Next a vast region extending from Jerusalem all the way to Illyricum was literally saturated with the Gospel, so much so that Paul declared that there was no more room in the area for the evangelistic dimension of his apostolic ministry (see Rom. 15:18-23).

Spreading of the gospel has continued to make progress through the centuries. In fact, it has gone so far that today every nation on Earth has at least a handful of Christians. Satan, with his bruised head, has not been able to withstand the advancing army of the Lord of lords. For the last 2,000 years he has been retreating rather than expanding his dominion. The day is fast approaching when he will be dealt the final blow, when "the God of peace will . . . crush Satan under your feet" (Rom. 16:20). On that day the will of God will be done *all over* the Earth as it is done in heaven.

This is the rematch I have been describing. I call it a rematch because it will involve the original contenders: human beings and the devil himself. Just like their predecessor in the Garden, women will play a central role. Except that this time, as God has predicted, Eve's daughters will win.

Where Satan's Head Will Be Crushed

The showdown is fast approaching, and it will take place inside the 10/40 Window.[1] I see three reasons for this.

1. **Location.** The Garden, the place where Satan scored first, was inside the 10/40 Window. Most scholars place the garden in the region where Iraq and Iran are today. This is one of the least receptive regions to the gospel. Being one of the places where Satan is most firmly entrenched, it will most likely also be where he will make his *last* stand.
2. **The condition of women.** The place on Earth where they are most degraded, disgraced, debased and deprived is inside the 10/40 Window, especially in militant Muslin nations where the desire of women is absolutely at the caprice of men who rule over them in the most dictatorial manner.
3. **Scriptural evidence.** Psalm 68 describes a decisive encounter between God and evil forces, in which women play a key role. The internal evidence in this Psalm points to the 10/40 Window as the battleground.

Looking at Psalm 68
Psalm 68 opens with battle lines clearly drawn: "Let God arise, let His enemies be scattered; and let those who hate Him flee

before Him" (v. 1). It closes with a majestic description of all the kingdoms of the earth singing praises to Him, "Sing to God, O kingdoms of the earth; sing praises to the Lord" (v. 32).

This change from open defiance to total submission is accomplished when "The Lord gives the command; the women who proclaim the good tidings are a great host: Kings of armies flee, they flee" (v. 11,12),[2] and as a result, God "scattered the peoples who delight in war" (v. 30).

This victory is so impressive that even Egypt—the cultural capital of Islam—sends envoys and Ethiopia, the site of systematic persecution of Christians, turns to God: "Envoys will come out of Egypt; Ethiopia will quickly stretch out her hands to God" (v. 31).

This psalm provides specific clues as to the location for this battle. The site is described as a combination of desert (v. 4), parched land (v. 6) and wilderness (v. 7). The mention of Judah, Zebulun and Naphtali (v. 27) places it in modern-day land of

We can confidently conclude that this battle, the ultimate rematch, will take place in the Middle East, inside the 10/40 Window.

Israel (v. 8). Mention of Sinai (v. 8), Egypt and Ethiopia (v. 31) expand the theater to the entire Middle East.

The reference to the kingdoms of the earth praising God after He had shattered "the head of . . . him who goes on in his guilty deeds" (v. 21) points in the direction that this is the final showdown, not just another war. We can confidently conclude that this battle, the ultimate rematch, will take place in the Middle East, inside the 10/40 Window.

The First All-Female Army

An all-female army plays a key role in this victory. God's enemies are completely defeated by "The Lord [when He] gives the command; [and all of a sudden] the women who proclaim the good tidings [become] are a great host [army]: Kings of armies flee, they flee" (Ps. 68:11,12).

The idea of women *who proclaim glad tidings* defeating evil kings is so extraordinary that to make sure this novel point is not lost the next verse reiterates, "She who remains at home will divide the spoil!" (v. 12). Spoils always belong to the victor.

Surprise As a Key

God uses the element of surprise. "When you lie down among the sheepfolds, you are like the wings of a dove covered with silver, and its pinions with glistening gold" (v. 13). As we saw in the opening chapter of this book, this verse compares the warring women to doves lying down on sheepfolds, their wings covered with silver and their pinions adorned with gold. As striking as this sounds, the actual scene was made intentionally dull—in fact, camouflaged by God so as not to lose the element of surprise.

Sheepfolds are sheepskins used to cover the floor inside a tent. They also double as seats and beds. Even if they came from a white sheep, after a period of use their color turns to gray. If silver-colored doves are placed on gray sheepfolds, they become inconspicuous for lack of contrast. Even the gold rings on their pinions do not attract attention because the doves lie on them.[3]

What we have here is women camouflaged as doves lying low with a treasure hidden underneath. The story of the doves reflects perfectly the reality of Muslim women today inside the 10/40 Window. The question is not will God release them as his mighty army, but how soon will they be released?

Looking at Zalmon

The next verse states, "When the Almighty scattered the kings there, it was snowing in Zalmon" (v. 14). What is the meaning of the snow, and why is Zalmon mentioned?

If multitudes of doves, with gold on their pinions, descend on an area, the place will look as if it is covered with snow. This happened in a location identified as Zalmon. This little-known elevation holds an important key, as we will soon see.

Abimelech's Defeat

Abimelech, the son of Gideon through one of his concubines, made Zalmon infamous. This evil character conspired with the inhabitants of Shechem—his hometown—against his deceased father's 70 legitimate sons and killed them in order to rule (see Judg. 8:32—9:6). Eventually a dispute arose between him and the people of Shechem. Abimelech besieged it, defeated its army and murdered most of its inhabitants (see Judg. 9:43-45).

However, a thousand men and women fled to a fortified tower. At that moment Abimelech climbed Mount Zalmon to show his army how to cut branches from the trees. Once they had enough firewood they transported it to the lower chamber of the tower. They set it on fire and burnt alive one thousand men and women (see Judg. 9:49). This was a cruel and vile act. The killing of non-warring civilians, especially women, amounted to genocide.

Next, Abimelech went to Thebez, a nearby town, and captured it, but some of the people also took refuge in another tower. He decided to burn them alive, just as he had done to the people in Shechem. However, as Abimelech approached the tower, a woman threw a millstone that landed on his head, "crushing his skull" (Judg. 9:53). As he lay moribund, he was more distressed by the fact that a woman had brought him down than he was concerned about his impending death. Consequently he commanded his armor bearer to "draw your sword and kill me, lest it be said of me: 'A woman slew him' " (Judg. 9:54).

Pride and the Fall

The reference to Mount Zalmon ties the events in Psalm 68 to the final crushing of Satan's head and the role women will play in it. The parallels are significant. Abimelech, the personification of evil, had his head crushed by a woman. In the same way that Abimelech despised women, the devil has also singled them out for harsher treatment. By showing his army how to cut branches that could then be used as firewood to turn an otherwise impregnable tower into a human pyre, he transformed a common tree into a devastating new weapon. This is similar to how Satan turned the tree in the Garden into a lethal weapon. Undoubtedly, his victory at Shechem gave him great confidence. Yet when he tried the same ploy a second time, a woman crushed his head before he had a chance to repeat it.

Likewise, Satan appears to be ahead of the game right now because Eve's transgression has resulted in a significant oppression of women. Consequently, he does not feel threatened by their lowly state, especially inside the 10/40 Window where so many of them are imprisoned in towers built with the stones and mortar of religious fanaticism. Satan succeeded once and, like Abimelech, he believes he can do it again, except that his head will be soon crushed. This will take him by surprise because the tower where Satan holds people captive will provide the impetus for the stone that will do the crushing.

Islam's Greatest Vulnerability

One of Islam's greatest social weaknesses is its treatment of women. They constitute 50 percent of the Muslim world and have been pushed down to a station so low that they have nothing else to lose. When half the people in a movement—no matter how powerful it is—are in a hopeless position due to something immutable such as their gender, they become a loose thread in its social fabric.

This is a thread that if pulled will unravel the whole tapestry of that society. This is the spiritual insight that Aglow International received in 1995.[4] Consequently, multitudes of women all over the world have focused their prayers and intercession on the 10/40 Window. They believe that at any time God will pull the female thread, and the social fabric of Islam will unravel.

Desperate people will do desperate things to change a desperate situation. Like the Israelites in Egypt—pushed to the limit by powerful oppressors and with no human hope in sight—women inside Islam could end up emulating the Israelites who "cried out; and their cry for help because of their bondage rose up to God" (Exod. 2:23).

God has a solid record of hearing the cry of hurting people, beginning with Hagar when she fled into the wilderness, pregnant with Ishmael. Could it be that her descendants, the women in Islam, out of desperation, will soon call upon God and will become a great host of female evangelists? I firmly think so.

A Preemptive Strike

The allusion to snow falling on Mount Zalmon appears to be a reference to a preemptive strike by God. Mount Zalmon is where Abimelech cut branches to set the tower on fire. However, if heavy snow were to fall at that precise moment, he would have failed to carry out his diabolic plans, because snow has a tendency to render branches unsuitable for immediate use as fire-wood!

The parallel to the eventual crushing of Satan's head inside the 10/40 Window, using women whom he believes pose no threat on account of their lowly station, cannot be clearer!

Why Women?

Why would God use women for such a decisive battle? It is simple: The *opening* round of the fight involved the devil and a woman, not a man. Consequently, it is logical to conclude that the *last* round of the final face-off should also include women.

Pointing to the fact that Eve lost the first round, some people might conclude that women should not be involved in this kind of confrontation. But haven't they ever heard the word "rematch"?

In Genesis 3:15, God Himself announces a rematch and He states that the woman and her seed will be part of it. Psalm 68 provides an abundance of detail as to how and where it will happen.

Another reason to accept God's choice of women is simply because He is God, and as such, He has the right to do as He wishes. This is what the reference to Bashan in the Psalms points to: "A mountain of God is the mountain of Bashan. A mountain of many peaks is the mountain of Bashan" (Ps. 68:15).

Interestingly enough, God calls Bashan a mountain of many peaks. Bashan, however, is not a mountain at all, but a high plateau with no peaks, much less "many peaks." In this section, God speaks to mountains that have peaks, "Why do you look with envy, O mountains with many peaks, at the mountain which God has desired for His abode?" (Ps. 68:15,16).

This seems to be a rebuke to those who object to God's choice of women for this important final thrust. If He chooses to call a high plateau a mountain and to ascribe many peaks to it, He is God and He can do it any time He wants.

Some people may say, "But women have never fought a war by themselves. War is a man thing." To that God might reply with something like this: "Have you forgotten that I am the God who created all things? If I can make the walls of a sea stand or turn a valley of dry bones into an army, I can choose to use women as an army."

Centuries of oppression will come to an end, and the beauty and the power of women will be on display just like the gold on the pinions of doves in flight.

Just like Peter who asked, "Lord, and what about this man?" (John 21:21), many people may expect an answer, but God will give them none. Instead, God will reply in the same manner Jesus did: "What is that to you? You follow me!" (John 21:22).

God's Plan

Abimelech never thought that he could be harmed by a woman when he was so close to annihilating his enemies. But quite unexpectedly a woman found the will to fight rather than to helplessly wait for her demise and wrought an unexpected victory!

This is the victorious outcome God has in store for the culmination of the rematch between the serpent and the woman and her seed. Centuries of oppression will come to an end, and the beauty and the power of women will be on display just like the gold on the pinions of doves in flight.

The issue is not *if* but *when*. To that effect there is a restoration process in motion that will reach its climax when women minister side by side with men (maidservants and bond servants, sons and daughters) as predicted by Joel (see Joel 2: 28,29). This process calls for the restoration of men as a prerequisite for women to be restored because the heavenly Commander in Chief wants to make sure that during the culmination of the rematch men will not fail women the way Adam failed Eve. Let us take a look at this in the next chapter.

Notes

1. The 10/40 Window is a missiological term that describes the region of the world that is located between 10 degrees north and 40 degrees north of the Equator and stretches from West Africa to East Asia. Inside the window falls the majority of the nations that are still unevangelized, most of which are Muslim nations.
2. The reference to women is not present in all translations. However, the original Hebrew indicates that this verse is speaking about women through the use of the *feminine plural* (not the masculine plural) participle.
3. Pinions are the longest feathers in the wings of doves.
4. This spiritual insight was received at the Aglow International Conference, Long Beach, CA, October 1995.

CHAPTER EIGHT

THE RESTORATION OF MEN AND WOMEN

God has been actively involved in restoration since Satan deceived Adam and Eve, beginning with the first animals He sacrificed to make clothes to cover their nakedness and culminating with the shedding of Jesus' blood to atone for the sins of the world. However, the most intense period of restoration has been reserved for the end times, prior to the final confrontation with the evil one.

There are two major prophecies that describe the restoration of women in the context of the establishment of God's kingdom on Earth. One has to do with the advent of the Messiah and the crushing of Satan's head; the other involves the outpouring of the Holy Spirit upon all humankind to liberate large numbers of captives from Satan's spiritual dungeons.

The first is found in Genesis 3:15 and has already been quoted extensively in previous chapters. The second is quoted by Peter in Acts 2:17-21,34,35:

> "And it shall be in the last days," God says, "That I will pour forth of My Spirit upon all mankind; and your sons and your daughters shall prophesy, and your young men shall see visions, and your old men shall dream dreams; even upon My bondslaves, both men and women, I will in those days pour forth of My Spirit. And they shall prophesy. And I will grant wonders in the sky above, and signs on the earth beneath, blood, and fire, and vapor of smoke. The sun shall be turned into darkness, and the moon into blood, before the great and glorious day of the Lord shall come. And it shall be, that everyone who calls on the name of the Lord shall be saved."
>
> The Lord said to my lord, "Sit at My right hand, until I make Thine enemies a footstool for thy feet."

Four Similarities and a Major Misunderstanding

Both of these Old Testament prophecies quoted in Acts were uttered at the onset of important dispensations and the fulfillment of each one is decisive for the Church's ultimate victory over Satan. They also have four impressive characteristics.

1. God is speaking rather than having a prophet prophesy (see 1 Pet. 1:20,21).
2. They were given when God launched divine counterattacks (the announcement of the Redeemer in Genesis 3:15 and the founding of the Church in Acts chapter 2) in retaliation for major satanic assaults that created the false impression of a diabolical victory (the Fall in the Garden and the crucifixion of Jesus at Calvary).
3. Both utterances foretell the eventual defeat of the devil—the bruising of his head in the first one (see Gen. 3:15) and the turning of him and his demons into a footstool for Jesus' feet in the other (see Acts 2:34,35).
4. Both depict women in prominent roles—carrying the seed that will defeat Satan in one instance and prophesying alongside men in a worldwide multilevel thrust aimed at freeing Satan's prisoners in the other.

We often assume that these extraordinary utterances have been *completely* fulfilled. Even though a significant amount of fulfillment has taken place, the bulk is yet to come. This is an important distinction because of the role assigned to women in both situations.

Victory in the Spirit Realm

Let us first examine the crushing of Satan's head.

It is true that Satan was fatally wounded when Christ shed His precious blood on the cross, descended into Hades and rose victoriously after asserting His authority over the devil and his demons (see Eph. 4:8-10). However, this does not constitute the final round but rather a very important opening match.

(1 Corinthians 15:24-26 [*NIV*] reads: "The end will come, when [Christ] hands over the kingdom to God the Father after He has destroyed all dominion, authority and power. For He must reign until He has put all His enemies under His feet.")

Christ's death paid the penalty for our sins, voiding the hostile decree (see Col. 2:14) the devil held against us and opening a sure way for God (see John 14:6).

However, Christ's victory on the cross, at the precise moment of its inception, affected primarily Satan and his demons, whom Christ disarmed and "made a public spectacle" (Col. 2:15, *NKJV*).

Such an outcome left no doubt in the spiritual realm that Jesus is the victor and Satan is the defeated one. Angels in heaven saw it happen, and demons in hell were subjugated by Him. No one in the heavenly places was left unaware that Satan had lost big-time.

Although mortally wounded at Calvary, Satan is still blinding the eyes of people to the light of the gospel.

Nevertheless, most of the captives on Earth—then and now—needed to be told of the freedom obtained through Jesus' blood. Because Satan has no intention of releasing his prisoners without a fight, Jesus' last official act was to commission His disciples to go to the ends of the Earth to announce His eternal pardon (see Acts 1:5,8).

Alive and Well on Planet Earth

The fact that the Church is called to struggle "against the powers, against the world forces of this darkness" and to take up "the shield of faith with which to extinguish the flaming missiles of the evil one" (see Eph. 6:12,16) shows that Satan's head has not yet been crushed, at least not to the point of completely disabling him; nor has his kingdom on Earth been dismantled. First Corinthians 15:25 (*NIV*) declares that Christ "must reign until He has put all His enemies under His feet."

Although mortally wounded at Calvary, Satan is still blinding the eyes of people to the light of the gospel (see 2 Cor. 2:11; 4:4). He would not be able to deceive people if he was out of commission. Paul testified to this when he said, "And the God of peace will [future tense] soon crush Satan under your feet" (Rom. 16:20). The tangible evidence of satanic entrenchment all over the world is proof that the *final* blow to Satan's head is yet to come.

Our Ignorance

Ignoring this point gives the devil a tremendous advantage. By assuming that he is not a threat to us, or to the proclamation of the gospel, he is able to go by stealth. Worse yet, the role of women in the great rematch is overlooked. Since it will take the entire Church to crush Satan's head, *and half of the Church is women*, they need to be brought up to par. This is where the restoration process comes in.

Joel Misunderstood

A similar misunderstanding can also happen regarding Joel's prophecy. Joel spoke of the Spirit of God being poured upon *all flesh*. "All flesh" means the population of the whole world; however, as of today only a portion has been touched by the Spirit of God. Furthermore, women are not partnering with men in ministry ("sons and daughters . . . bondslaves, both men and women prophesying") in the midst of a worldwide harvest of souls. In *most* countries no massive outpouring has happened, and women are still considered second-class citizens both in the society at large and often in the Church.

Peter did not present what happened on Pentecost as the ultimate fulfillment of Joel's prophecy, but as something consistent with the events foretold by the prophet, of which the outpouring of the Holy Spirit was the *initiation*. It is definitely a *process* designed to continually increase until it reaches a crescendo at the culmination of the restoration process.

This process currently underway around the world involves several distinct elements of restoration: intercession, spiritual warfare, unity, evangelism, men and, ultimately, women.

Intercession

As we enter the new millennium, intercessors who constitute God's Strategic Weapons And Tactics teams have arisen around the world. The emergence of these SWAT units is such a new phenomenon that 10 years ago they were virtually unknown. Most observers identify the debut of these SWAT teams with the convening of a group of on-site intercessors by C. Peter Wagner during the Lausanne II Congress in the Philippines in 1989.[1] More than a decade later, every significant activity in Christendom includes intercessors before, during and after the event. Definitely, intercession has been restored and is here to stay.

Spiritual Warfare

Another area of restoration involves the rediscovery of spiritual warfare as a biblical weapon. Not too long ago the prevailing posi-

tion was "Ignore the devil and he shall flee." This is the exact opposite of the admonition given in James 4:7: "Resist the devil and he
will flee from you." Since Lausanne II, the Church has awakened
to the biblical mandate that we are to stand firm against the
schemes of the evil one and that we must resist him *until he flees*.

Unity

Christians have always believed in unity, but until recently it has
been an ideal to be pursued rather than an attainable goal.
Today the expression "One church made up of many congregations" is first coming to reflect the normal state of affairs in
cities all over the world.

Evangelism

The Church is also rediscovering a compelling evangelistic
vision as embodied in the city-reaching movement. When John
Dawson wrote *Taking Our Cities for God*[2] in the late '80s, the concept was so challenging and novel that most people had no
frame of reference for it.

Today, city-reaching movements thrive all over the world,
and some are beginning to evolve into nation-reaching thrusts.
The issue is no longer if, but rather when, our cities and nations
will be reached for Christ. George Otis, Jr.'s video *Transformation*
has brought home the point that cities can be reached, and better yet, that some are being transformed.

Men and Women

The restoration of men is crucial to the eventual restoration of
women. For most of the twentieth century, men, particularly
American men, have not been spiritual leaders or protectors,
especially at home. Many of them have shown a marked inabili-
ty to relate intimately to the women in their lives, whether they
be their mothers, sisters or wives.

Many of those roots go back to the two world wars. No nation can afford to ship overseas the bulk of its male population between the ages of 18 and 35 for as long as five years without suffering a significant social disruption. This is compounded when it is accompanied by the massive relocation of women from home to factories to perform traditional male jobs. The bonding that occurs in combat situations, something that most men in World War I and II experienced, further accentuates the gender gap.

Following Armistice Day, hundreds of thousands of men returned home to their mothers, sisters, girlfriends and wives—all at once! They came back to women who had also been socially uprooted, leaving both groups without traditional moorings. Consequently, making proper attachment or reattachment turned out to be very difficult or, in many cases, impossible. After a while it became easier for men to give up or to bond with other men, something they had been doing while overseas. In the end, this hurt their marriages, their homes and eventually their children. Remember, in the last century, this severe social disruption happened not once but twice.

The Volcano Finally Erupts

Even though on the surface life looked stable, there was a powerful undercurrent that came to the surface when children born after World War II reached adolescence. In the '60s and '70s hippies and flower kids took defiantly to the streets in search of themselves. Traditional values were summarily spurned and rejected. Confused children criticized their unsure parents and, all of a sudden, two generations went over the edge with no rope to hold them from above and no safety net to catch them below.

Values such as commitment, chastity and loyalty were ripped from the soul of an entire generation. Men's failure to exercise their God-given role as protectors and providers affected wives and children, causing them to lose security and damaging their identity. Many women clung to the hollow tree of feminism in a futile attempt to find a mooring in the midst of a cataclysmic social typhoon. As a result, the social fiber of the home was severely damaged and the backbone of the family was fractured, covering millions of people with the filthy residue of grimy guilt.

Men are designed to be protectors and providers. Failure to be either creates a void right at the center of their identities.

It is precisely this unmerciful social chaos that produced the need for men to be restored. The Promise Keepers organization is one example of the many vehicles God has been using to rebuild men as we enter a new century.

Men are designed to be protectors and providers. Failure to be either creates a void right at the center of their identities. When identity is compromised in this way, self-worth suffers bankruptcy and hopelessness takes over. The biblical message of repentance and restitution of ministries such as Promise Keepers is being enthusiastically embraced by millions of men because they see this as the only way out. Most of the more than 3 million men who have participated in stadium events have been transformed. By reclaiming their God-given roles, they began to rebuild the hedge of protection that is vital for female restoration to take place.

The Restoration of Women

The restoration of women is the central message of this book. This is definitely the last and most dynamic frontier before the final blow to Satan's head brings us full circle.

Women have always been involved in Kingdom matters in the forefront of God's work. When men were somewhere else, women were "manning" the trenches in the Church. Women were so involved that if all of a sudden they were to quit, most congregations would have folded overnight!

However, women's potential in the Kingdom has been negatively affected by the lack of protection that men are supposed to provide. Like Eve in the Garden, women today have stood up to the devil but have not been able to crush him.

Rebuilding Men First

It may seem contradictory that the restoration of men would result in greater freedom and effectiveness for women. But this ceases to be inharmonious when we understand that men are uniquely designed to provide protection for women. In the same manner that men are incomplete without women, women without men's protection become more vulnerable to the schemes of their archenemy. Eve's fall was made possible by Adam's neglect of his responsibility as protector.

Men as Restorers

Men are instructed to do the opposite of what Adam did when sin first touched him through Eve. Adam disowned Eve as his wife, and in an act of total cowardice told God, "The woman whom thou gavest to be with me, she gave me of the tree" (Gen. 3:12, *KJV*). In other words, Adam is pointing his finger and saying, "She made me do it!" He simply chose to forget that she was bone of his bones and flesh of his flesh and renounced his oneness with the woman God had fashioned for him.

In 1 Timothy 2:8-13 Paul commands husbands to do the exact opposite by standing with their wives in public (v. 8), by making provision for their godliness to be evident (v. 9) and by teaching them what they know in an intimate setting, the home (v. 11). In other words, Paul is saying, "Your wife is your suitable help, your indispensable complement, so make her look better, feel better and understand better." This is the opposite of what Adam did in the Garden.

Furthermore, in Ephesians chapter 5, Paul tells husbands that they must humble themselves before their wives (v. 21), they must give themselves to their wives as Christ gave Himself to the Church (v. 25) and they must love their wives as much as they love their own bodies (v. 28). This passage complements 1 Timothy 2:8-13. As such, it validates the need for Christian men to remove the iniquity produced by Adam's response to Eve's transgression.

This is why the eventual restoration of women is dependent on the ongoing restoration of men, so that marriages will be able to reflect the intimacy first seen in the Garden when both genders walked and worked together in the presence of God. Men need to be able to see their wives as the focus of their love, honor and attention. To do so it is necessary to understand that men today are no different from Adam. They face the same challenges and are subject to similar limitations.

Let us see how this can be overcome, because the gender gap is what keeps Satan's empire standing. Nothing pleases the devil more than when men fail to be reconciled with women.

Notes

1. For a detailed account of how this came about, see C. Peter Wagner, *Prayer Shield* (Ventura, CA: Regal, 1992), p. 150.
2. John Dawson, *Taking Our Cities for God: How to Break Spiritual Strongholds* (Lake Mary, FL: Creation House, 1990).

CHAPTER NINE

MEN HAVE A LOT IN COMMON WITH ADAM

Lack of reconciliation between men and women is what keeps in place the worldwide system of lies the devil uses to dishonor women and to cripple men. It is imperative that we discover why it is not easy for men to understand women and what provision God has made to overcome this leftover from the Fall.

Adam never saw a woman until God deposited Eve in front of him. His initial perplexity, and especially the way he handled it, provides an important clue to understanding contemporary gender difficulties.

When Adam was presented with someone whom he knew nothing about, he tried to figure her out instead of asking questions. He went from the known—"you are bone of my bones and flesh of my flesh"—to the unknown—"you are a woman." The first part he understood; the second part left him clueless. Adam's approach matches men's general attitude toward women. Most men are like Adam, they are captivated by a woman's physical looks—flesh *of my flesh*—but tend to dump everything else under an all-inclusive label: "woman." They usually fail to realize that the content they do not see is far greater and more sophisticated than the container in front of them. Time and again, when men fail to fathom a female's actions or thoughts they settle it by stating, "Well, she is a woman, after all."

If men were to study the contour of a woman's soul with the same interest with which they scrutinize the shape of her body, there would be little misunderstanding between the sexes. Unfortunately, ignorance of what is inside a woman provides a lifeline for the bigotry that characterizes so many prejudicial responses to female actions and behavior.

If women are to be restored, it is essential that we find ways for men to not just admire their female counterparts, but also to accept them the way they are. A full-fledged acceptance of women will allow them to welcome the creative tension that comes when people connect who are sufficiently similar but different enough to stretch them out of their comfort zone.

Designed to Remain a Mystery

Women are like fascinating, intriguing, perplexing and at times confusing books. Every time men get to the last page and feel they have learned everything there is to learn, an entire new volume is added overnight!

Ironically, it is this unfathomable feminine dimension that makes women so desirable, because if men were able to understand them fully, they would become bored and try to redesign them. This is why men are instructed to live with women "in an understanding way" (1 Pet. 3:7). They must continuously study them and diligently observe them, not to invalidate or change what they do not comprehend, but to accept women the way they are.

> Ignorance of what is inside a woman provides a lifeline for the bigotry that characterizes so many prejudicial responses to female actions and behavior.

Many men do the exact opposite. They observe women long enough to come up with a list of what they perceive is wrong, according to a man's frame of reference; then they try to rebuild them according to male blueprints. After countless attempts to refashion women, men discover that women cannot be changed. Instead of accepting women as God has fashioned them, men become frustrated and hopeless. Men should consider another possibility: that women are different because they have not been created to serve men but to serve *with* them in a *complementary* capacity.

Wives to Be Honored

God is so serious about this that He has established severe penalties for men who do not live with their wives in an understanding way:

> You husbands likewise, live with your wives in an understanding way, as with a weaker vessel, since she is a woman; and grant her honor as a fellow heir of the grace of life, so that your prayers may not be hindered (1 Pet. 3:7).

Please notice the reference to women being coheirs of the grace of life. Men have no problem generously sharing the grace of God with women, but the *grace of life* Peter is talking about here is something else. It means that on this planet men and women are co-tenants, coheirs, cosigners and costewards. The bottom line is: Women have the same rights that men have.

Any man who disobeys this command will have his prayers hindered. God will not listen to men until they listen to their wives. On this issue, God has taken a strong position to ensure that women are properly treated.

God exhorts men to truly understand their female counterparts. Unfortunately, many times that knowledge stops at the outer limit of the female anatomy. A disturbingly large number of men make no unbiased attempt to learn what goes on inside a woman's soul, mind and heart. This attitude is at the very heart of the gender gap because no one can appreciate what he does not understand.

God's Commands for Men

Women are different, and the Bible states that the responsibility to understand them lies with men. In Deuteronomy 24:5, a husband is commanded to stay one year at home right after marriage for the purpose of making his new bride happy. In Ephesians 5:28, a husband is told to love his wife as much as he loves his own body. In Matthew 19:5, a man is instructed to leave his father and mother and to cleave to his wife until the two become one flesh. They become one when they achieve a new identity. Even though they remain two individuals, in marriage the two become one.

In each case, the primary responsibility for developing a pleasant home atmosphere is with the man rather than the woman. He is the one whom God charges with the responsibility of making her happy, loving her as he loves himself and cleaving to her until their new identity has been forged. This unity is so strong that, as far as God is concerned, it is indivisible.

Man's Need for Women

These commands would not be so prominently displayed in the Scriptures unless God sees a compelling need for them to be kept.

It is very important to underline the biblical perspective on this issue because so many women struggle with tremendous guilt when faced with serious problems in their marriages or families. They feel that they are the ones who have failed when in reality husbands share a significant responsibility for the outcome in any situation. This unhealthy false guilt has to be discarded.

However, what can be done when a husband does not cooperate? How can he be convinced *and transformed* by the scriptural truths and principles quoted in this chapter?

Two Commands, One Promise

One of the most enslaving assumptions is that for a struggling couple to be restored they must both undergo counseling together and agree to follow the prescribed advice. This is an ideal approach, but it is not the easiest way to restore a marriage.

God knew there would be a lack of cooperation between spouses during moments of crisis, so, as only God could do, He provided a dynamic solution. He gave men and women different commands but the same promise in order to make a marriage work. He told men to *love* their wives (see Eph. 5:28) and women to *honor* their husbands (1 Pet. 3:1,2). To love and to honor are different commands, yet each one carries the same promise: the restoration in the disobedient partner.

God established a wonderful principle: When a wife honors a husband who is disobedient to the Word that husband will be changed and become obedient (see 1 Pet. 3:1,2). God also determined that the spots and wrinkles in a wife's character will be eliminated when her husband chooses to love her (see Eph. 5:22-25).

This divine arrangement is similar to the double-brake system in cars. If one system fails the other one takes over in order to save the car from destruction. For women, the key is to be loved. For men, it is to be honored.

A Man's Craving for Respect

What a man needs the most is respect, most of all respect from his wife. This is why God instructs women to honor their husbands. For a man, love does not rate as high as respect. When someone refers to him as an honorable person, something vital is nurtured, and a jolt of pleasure travels the length and width of his soul. This is why he puts in long hours, endures difficulties and faces challenges at work beyond what his salary is worth. He craves the recognition it produces.

God tells wives to honor their husbands, because when they do this it causes their husbands to do *anything* for them, even to become obedient to the Word they are rebelling against (see 1 Pet. 3:1,2). To be honored by their wives is the highest desire men have. The reason behind this craving goes back to the moment of conception.

Women are different because they have not been created to serve men but to serve *with* them in a *complementary* capacity.

Every man is conceived and hosted for nine months inside a woman. As he is breast-fed and cared for by her, he attunes his ears and mind to the tone and cadence of her voice. When he becomes a toddler, she is the one who guides, corrects and instructs him. As he grows up, he becomes increasingly dependent on her approval and affirmation. This is clearly seen in the unique relationship that a son and a mother develop, a bond closer and far more intense than the one a boy has with his dad.

When a man gets married, the soul circuitry linking him to a woman is already in place, and the approval and honor of the wife becomes as vital to his sense of success as his mother's was while he was growing up. This is why God unabashedly assures women that they will change their husbands if they choose to honor them. Honor is what makes a man tick. In the same way that no one can live without oxygen, no man can go on in life without a minimal measure of honor.

Abram and Sarai

Two clear examples of this need for respect are found in Genesis chapters 12 and 20. Both involve Abram and Sarai.

Abram acted immorally when he twice lied to kings by presenting Sarai as his sister instead of the wife she was. There is no record of Sarai dishonoring Abram by exposing him as a deceiver even though what was at stake was her most precious virtue: sexual purity. However, when she became seriously endangered God intervened and delivered her as well as Abram.

This is consistent with the imagery used in 1 Peter 2:20,25:

> But if when you do what is right and suffer for it you patiently endure it, this finds favor with God . . . For you were continually straying like sheep, but now you have returned to the Shepherd and Guardian of your souls.

Peter presents a picture of righteous suffering patiently endured because God is the shepherd who cares for the needy sheep and the guardian who keeps the enemy away.

It is fitting that the next verse addresses the issue of wives, such as Sarai (later called Sarah), who must deal with disobedient husbands (see 1 Pet. 3:1-4). Submission, which is another way to say honoring, is presented as the way to change them. Furthermore, Old Testament women are used as examples, with Sarai's situation singled out as the premier illustration.

Today, Abram, who later became Abraham, is remembered as a man of renowned faith, courage and righteousness. I wonder how much of that was the result of Sarai's *less known but very heroic behavior*. Undoubtedly she needed faith, courage and righteousness to live in pagan courts where kings were after her, while at the same time her husband was more concerned with saving his own skin than he was with protecting his wife's virtue. Sarai changed Abram by honoring him even though he did not deserve or expect it. It works!

Honey Preferred over Vinegar

A drop of honey catches more flies than a barrel of vinegar. You do not believe this? Just look at some everyday situations and you will see.

For months, a wife I will call Kathy has pestered her husband to fix a leaky faucet in the house, but he keeps putting it off. One night at 3 A.M., in the midst of a severe storm, he receives a call from an elderly lady who lives on the other side of town. She needs help because her toilet has backed up and the house is a total mess. He promptly gets dressed, drives through flooded streets, fixes the problem and, overflowing with satisfaction, he returns home barely on time to shower and go to work.

Kathy is perplexed and fast approaching the threshold into "mad country." She cannot understand why her husband will put himself through so much trouble to do something so exhausting for a stranger while refusing day after day to complete a task as simple as fixing a faucet.

The reason is simple: the elderly lady most likely honored him by stressing how much she appreciated what he did and how she knew she could rely on him. In contrast, if he had ever fixed the faucet at home, Kathy would have said, "It is about time you did it!" Honey is definitely more appealing than vinegar.

God has empowered wives with the ability to honor their husbands and in so doing to change them for the better. Even though men may have intrinsic difficulties understanding and connecting with women, God has placed at the disposal of both of them the resources needed to bridge the gap. As we will see in the next chapter, a lack of intimacy between Noah and his wife allowed evil to spread all over the post-Flood world.

CHAPTER TEN

NOAH'S MISTAKE

Have you ever wondered why evil was able to manifest itself so soon after the Flood?

God does not make mistakes. He never miscalculates. If He sent the flood to purge a corrupt system and replace it with a healthier one, why did sin come back so soon? The answer has to do with a major mistake Noah made in relation with his wife.[1]

Prior to the Flood, marriage reflected the lack of equality in relationship between a man and woman that was the result of the Fall. Men did not walk side by side with their wives.

According to the biblical narrative, Noah entered the Ark first, followed by his sons, then by his wife and finally by his sons' wives. This order is mentioned twice (see Gen. 7:7,13). Notice that Noah's sons boarded before his wife did. This succession reflects the lower position assigned to her after the Fall.

After the Flood, as the waters receded, God prepared Noah to come out of the Ark. This was a momentous occasion because the *remnant* saved by God was to reconnect with the purified creation. To that effect, God gave Noah specific instructions on how to go about it.

Noah and his household were told by God to disembark in the order that existed in the Garden *before* the Fall. The Lord said to Noah: "Go out of the ark, you and your wife and your sons and your sons' wives" (Gen. 8:16). Look closely at how God placed Noah's wife next to him *and ahead of the children*. Sequential order is important in biblical narratives, especially when God is the one enunciating it.

When Noah Did Not Follow God's Order

Unfortunately, Noah did not follow God's instructions. The narrative in Genesis tells us, "Noah went out, and his sons and his wife and his sons' wives" (v. 18). He relegated his wife below the children, reflecting the old order rather than the new one. Almost immediately this would have tragic consequences.

Noah planted a vine, harvested its fruit, made wine, unfortunately got drunk and lay naked in his tent. When his son Ham saw him, he despised Noah and reported it to his brothers in a manner demeaning to Noah. This resulted in Ham's son, Canaan, being cursed by Noah after he learned what had happened. This curse, in turn, had catastrophic repercussions.

Could this have been avoided? Yes. Of course, Noah should never have gotten drunk in the first place. But beyond that there never would have been a curse if Noah's wife had been in the tent with him instead of Ham. For her to see him naked would not have been a problem. Most likely she would have covered him up, Noah would have slept off his stupor, and there would have been no backlash. But his wife probably was not there because she had been relegated to a secondary role. If Noah had obeyed God and left the Ark in the way prescribed by God, none of this would have happened.

> # In the same fashion that men are to protect women's minds, women are designed to protect men's hearts.

Intimacy a Must in Marriage

Intimacy in marriage, the closest relationship between genders, is vital. Without this closeness the image of God continues to be distorted on Earth, since both man and woman have been equally entrusted to maintain intimacy in their relationship. In addition, lack of intimacy opens the door to the enemy by rendering a key flank vulnerable.

In the same fashion that men are to protect women's minds, women are designed to protect men's hearts. Women are not necessarily more godly than men, but they are definitely more spiritual. They are able to perceive spiritual things with greater ease. The expression "suitable help" used by God to describe Eve in ancient Hebrew means "the revealer of the enemy."[2] Eve proved this when she identified Satan as the deceiver. Also, in the well-known biblical passage describing a virtuous woman, we are told that "the heart of her husband trusts in her" and as a result "he will have no lack of gain" (Prov. 31:11).

This is why Satan will do anything within his power to undermine and, if possible, destroy intimacy between men and women. The so-called social mandate, ruling over creation, was given to both the husband and the wife, and it was done in the specific context of marriage.

God instructed them to "be fruitful, multiply and subdue the earth" (Gen. 1:28). To be fruitful requires marriage. To multiply involves having children. To subdue the earth refers to joint ministry. The two of them were to work together, as one flesh, cleaving to each other, to subdue every living creature, including the serpent. This is no light matter: Adam failed to stand by Eve when the serpent came; the rest is sad history.

This is why it is foundational for men and women to be restored in their relationships. Otherwise, the devil will gain an entrance just as he did with Adam and Eve in the Garden and with Noah after the Flood. Intimacy is the key, and nowhere is intimacy better achieved and preserved than in a healthy marriage.

Today's Marriages on the Brink

As we cross the threshold into the new millennium, the institution of marriage is under severe attack. While this has always been the case, nowadays the assaults are so effective and of such magnitude that some people predict the end of marriage as we know it.

What is going on? Where does God stand in all of this?

Marriage is the most complex undertaking on Earth. It is the complete union—in soul, spirit and body—of two human beings who are totally different and in many cases direct opposites. Who devised this unique and at times puzzling relationship?

God is the one who created marriage. In fact, He likes marriage so much that He opened the Bible with a marriage and closed it with another one. He performed the first wedding in the Garden and He will preside over the wedding of Christ and the Church at the close of the ages. Jesus Himself performed what is believed to be His first miracle at a wedding. Several times afterward He used the imagery of marriage to teach the noblest truths

All through the Bible, God protects marriage by providing specific directives designed to preserve it and enrich it. Yes, God loves marriage, and He definitely stands behind it.

What God and the Devil Think

The opposite is also true: What God loves the devil hates. From the very beginning the evil one has been busy undermining, and whenever possible, defiling the union of man and woman. I suspect that three things constitute his main motivation for his unrelenting attack on marriages:

- Marriage, as God designed it, produces the most intimate union between two beings, and Satan's business is not uniting, it is dividing.
- The concept of love is so foreign and abhorrent to him—and nothing illustrates human love better than marriage—that destroying marriages is very high on Satan's priority list.

· When spouses call it quits, no matter the reason, the ones who suffer the greatest damage are the children. That is why the devil works so hard at destroying marriages, because when he succeeds he gets a bonus in the harm done to the next generation. This, in turn, has devastating consequences when those children get married and find themselves trapped inside the disabling maze of scar tissue left by their parents' divorce.

The Most Important Reason

However, there is another reason for marriage to be targeted and attacked by the enemy. It is strategic and has to do with prayer. The Lord Jesus made it clear that there is power when two (or three) agree in prayer (see Matt. 18:19,20). The most natural and intimate prayer pairing of people comes in marriage. If a husband and a wife, who share a house, a bed, a table and a family, exercise this power consistently, the kingdom of darkness will suffer terrible damage. Jesus told us that everything asked in such context of unity will be done by His Father in heaven. What a tremendous blank check He handed us!

God did not make a mistake when He created marriage. In fact He stated that it was a necessity. Just look at what God said in Genesis: "It is not good for the man [or woman] to be alone" (Gen. 2:18). He knew what He was doing then, and He knows what He is doing now.

Restored marriages are at the very top of God's list because men and women need to minister together just as Adam and Eve did in the Garden before the Fall. They need to walk side by side, in unity, just as God intended Noah to walk with his wife after the Flood. No matter how impossible things look, God is able and God is willing. We need to believe Him.

To find the basis for our faith to be activated, we need to gain a better understanding of what a unique gift a spouse is. This is the subject of the next chapter.

Notes
1. Ted Hahs, our chief intercessor at Harvest Evangelism, provided me with this insight which he, in turn, got from an intercessor in Modesto, California.
2. Frank T. Seekins, *Hebrew Word Pictures*, (Phoenix, AZ: Living Word Pictures, n.d.) pp. 1, 72, 73.

CHAPTER ELEVEN

HEADSHIP: FREEDOM FOR WOMEN

Your spouse is the only personal gift God will ever give to you. He has given and will continue to give you many gifts; however, of those gifts, only your spouse is uniquely and exclusively designed for your personal enjoyment. Your salvation is the most precious present, but millions of people have it. Your job is another gift, but eventually someone else will pick up where you leave off. Your children have been entrusted to you for a season, but sooner or later they will leave the family nest.

However, when it comes to your spouse, God has created a person exclusively for you to enjoy in the context of marriage. He or she belongs to you and no one else *until death do you part*. He or she is a gift for life. No one else is entitled to that person but you.

When God created Ruth, my wife, He was thinking exclusively of me as far as marriage is concerned. Her sense of perfection is an ideal balance for my liberal visionary drive, and her eye for detail enriches and completes the ever-growing big picture I forever find myself drawing. It is incredible that God created and entrusted me with such a person for a lifetime. She is mine and no one else's. I am hers and no one else's.

Your spouse deserves the best from you because no one can make you as happy as he or she can. Your spouse can give you sexual pleasure without guilt, understanding without patronizing, companionship without a price, children without shame.

Every time we love our spouses, God smiles on us. As a husband and wife lovingly embrace each other, the mystery of marriage with all its beauty adds another light to this dark planet.

Yes, God has given us a unique and personal gift in our spouses. To make sure this extraordinary union works, He has delineated clearly the roles and positions that each person is to have. In such context headship comes to the forefront.

Understanding Headship

What is headship? The term elicits unpleasant images of wives being told to submit to nonsensical husbands. It evokes visions of husbands being granted a license to abuse wives and scar children with the hot iron of unreasonableness. It projects the picture of wounded women deciding to fly solo in life and in ministry primarily because they have come to resent men. This move inevitably puts them in a place where they can be further defiled and, in many cases, destroyed because the system has been designed and run by men. Whether the woman aspires to be an executive or a minister, the odds against her are phenomenal. Many times they are made even higher by a faulty understanding of what headship is all about.

Headship in the Bible

It is interesting to notice that the term "headship" does not appear in the Bible. It is, however, a doctrine drawn from several passages. The roots go back to the order of creation. Adam was created first, and with that came certain privileges and responsibilities. Due to Eve's transgression, following the Fall, he was entrusted with additional jurisdiction. Even though Christ leveled the playing field at Calvary there is enough residue around to easily confuse us.

The classical section on headship in the New Testament is found in 1 Corinthians 11, where Paul holds an extensive discussion on male/female roles and positions. The central passage reads:

> But I want you to understand that Christ is the head of every man [husband], and the man [husband] is the head of a woman [wife], and God is the head of Christ (1 Cor. 11:3).[1]

When we see that the man is the head of a woman as Christ is the head of every man, at first glance it seems that women are held in an inferior position. Is this really what Paul is saying?

This particular verse presents us with the same challenge we face regarding the order of creation as it differs from the order in which sin entered the world. What can be more absolute than Christ's position over every man? Christ is superior. He is the boss. He is the one in charge. He has supreme authority. If this is the basis for headship, then women must remain in a subservient position.

Inside the Trinity

Before we jump to any conclusions, let us back up a moment and apply the same logic to the statement, "and God is the head of Christ." If we are thinking about hierarchy, we run into a serious theological problem. God the Father is not superior to Christ the Son, nor does the Son rank higher than the Spirit. We know that there are no hierarchies inside the Trinity.

The Greek word for "head" is *kephale*, which can mean either ruler/leader or source/origin. In this passage it makes sense to read it as source or origin, as well as a leader, since it fits better with the reference to members of the Trinity as well as with the overall context.

Among other reasons, we know that God is the source/leader of Christ because He sent Jesus into the world (see John 3:16; 5:19). In the same manner, Christ, the second Adam, is the head/origin/source of every new man in the Church in the same fashion that Adam was in the natural order.

Man As Spiritual Source

Man as the source/origin of the woman also carries into the spiritual realm. Christ began with 12 *male* apostles. Even though roles and offices were later assigned to women as well, it began with men when Christ laid the foundation for the new order, the Church.

To emphasize the absolute interdependence between men and women, Paul brought it back to the issue of origins when he said, "For as the woman originates from the man, so also the man has his birth through the woman; and all things originate from God" (1 Cor. 11:12). There is no room for male superiority here, since men and women cannot exist without each other.

This interdependence is consistent with the thrust to restore both genders to their pre-Fall position. In the Garden, Adam was created first, and as such, he was given a role as protector when God handed down the prohibition not to eat from the tree. But it is also true that Adam by himself was "not good" (Gen. 2:18). It was Eve's creation that enabled *both* of them to rule over all creation since the command was not given until after she was created. In Genesis 1:28, the Hebrew verb commanding Adam and Eve to rule over the creation is *plural*—it is a command given to both the man and the woman, which means that the woman rules alongside her husband (see also Gen. 2:18).[2]

What Greeks Thought of Women

It is important to bear in mind that first-century culture perceived women as inferior to men to the point of theorizing that females were created from lower forms of life rather than from man himself. In such a context Paul's argument that men and women are intrinsically linked—like head and body—is not a putdown on women, but a significant step up.

In fact, the word "submission" is never used in this section of Scripture from which we derive much of our current thinking on headship. 1 Corinthians 7 is devoted to presenting women in equal partnership and status with men. Paul makes the following strong points:

1. A man has a right to a wife as much as a wife has a right to a husband (see v. 2).
2. Both husbands and wives must fulfill their sexual obligation (see v. 3) because their bodies belong to each other rather than to themselves (see v. 4). If a

couple deprives themselves sexually it should only be by *mutual* consent (see v. 5). These are extraordinary statements issued at a time when women had no rights whatsoever!

Conditioning for the Rematch

We must understand that this passage, so often used to put women down, rather lifts them back to the level Eve had before the Fall. The devil has a unique ability to cloud our understanding of the Scriptures, allowing us to reach wrong conclusions, as in the case of the enmity between the women and him. He is the one threatened, not the women. This wrong view is also evident in the issue of women needing instruction, which men sometimes use to put down women (see 1 Tim. 2:12-14). The devil wants us to see these passages in a restrictive rather than a restorative light.

In the same fashion that a fighter who trains for a rematch seeks to obtain the same or higher level of conditioning he had in the first match, God is reconditioning men and women for the upcoming showdown. In the Garden, Adam and Eve were more than two separate individuals; they were a couple united in matrimony who had cleaved and become one. Marriage is at the center of this picture. God's goal is that man and woman will not only be restored to what they had in the Garden, but that they will now be in an even stronger position.

The Way Adam and Eve Were

What was the status of man and woman in the Garden?

God told Adam and Eve:

Be fruitful and multiply, and fill the earth, and subdue it; and rule over the fish of the sea and over the birds of the sky, and over every living thing that moves on the earth. . . . I have given you every plant . . . and every tree which has fruit . . . it shall be food for you (Gen. 1:28,29).

God's instructions reflect three concentric circles. Within the first circle, the very center, are the couple and their offspring. The next circle outward is what they are to rule over, which is every form of animal life. Then comes the outermost circle, which contains God's provision for them as well as for all that they are to rule over.

God is the one who created marriage. In fact, He likes marriage so much that He opened the Bible with a marriage and closed it with another one.

It is important to notice the central role assigned to the couple and subsequently to the family. Adam and Eve were to minister together and, when children came, to do this as a family. Nowadays we have dichotomized ministry and family. This plays straight into the hands of the devil, who wants to keep men and women as well as parents and children separated in order to eliminate the synergism their combination produces.

To correct this, the New Testament overflows with teaching regarding the restoration of women, the sanctity of marriage and the partnership between parents and children. Ministry, like in the Garden, is to be a family affair, not a separate and at times competing profession. When we dichotomize family and ministry, the two become adversaries and eventually enemies. In the end, they devour intimacy in marriage and ultimately the children's destiny.

Outside the Home

The principle of headship becomes destructive when an adversarial approach is taken to the male-female relationship in marriage. Interaction between husband and wife is meant to be an edifying and uplifting relationship. Those who embrace male supremacy crush women and lose 50 percent of the workforce, and in the process, they maim themselves since "It is not good for the man to be alone." Those who sponsor a feminist approach leave women exposed, like Eve was in the Garden, since women cannot stand up to the devil alone. Those who seek a compromise by saying that headship is legitimate at home but not in ministry take away the key contribution of headship: protection. Where do women need protection the most, at home or outside of the home? Obviously, they need it more when they are out in the world.

Headship in Ministry

I believe that the whole issue of headship in ministry can be settled if we take a global perspective rather than a balkanized one. God has entrusted men with protecting women, and women with complementing men. In the same fashion that children cannot be born unless men and women engage themselves at the most intimate level, likewise ministry cannot reach its intended summit without a similar partnership between genders, especially between husbands and wives.

When we see ministry as an extension of family life (see 1 Tim. 3:1-13), the dichotomizing of headship becomes a mute point. If men are entitled to headship in the home and ministry life is to be an extension of family life, then they have the same responsibility in ministry that they have at home. This is very important because men tend to loaf when it comes to spiritual matters. Even in ministry, they usually lean toward vision and drive, but fall pitifully short in the areas of care and nurture. Women, as I have noted in previous chapters, tend to excel in the deeper levels of spirituality. Ministering as a couple solves the problem.

What About Singles?

Singleness can be for a season or for a lifetime. In either case, it is a divine calling. Paul teaches that an "unmarried [person] is concerned about the things of the Lord" (1 Cor. 7:32) and that singleness provides a setting for "undistracted devotion to the Lord" (1 Cor. 7:35). Singles have an option that married people no longer have: to devote all of their energy and time to serving Him.

I remember during my single years, even though my friends and I were swamped with school and work responsibilities, how energizing it was to allocate every extra minute to the Lord and to the church. After a grueling day in school or at work we would freely and enthusiastically get together to spend part or all of the night in prayer. Sometimes we would spend the entire weekend preaching in faraway places. We never had to worry about domestic duties, we were single and devoted to the Lord and His work. It was a most fruitful season.

Singleness does not have to mean being alone and isolated. Jesus was single and yet He struck a perfect balance. When He was not with the Father, in prayer (sometimes all-night prayer times), He was surrounded by people to whom He ministered or who ministered to Him.

The dual focus on God and on people that Jesus modeled for us is designed to shape our character in an extraordinary way. If singleness is for a season it will prepare the person for marriage by developing a balanced approach to both vertical (with God) and horizontal (with people) relationships. If singleness is to be a life-long calling, it will protect the person from harmful distractions.

Whether the person is single or married, a healthy family setting is needed. Paul highlights the close interpersonal relationships that must characterize singles in his letter to Timothy, who was also a single minister. Paul calls Timothy "my son" (1 Tim. 1:18) and instructs him to appeal to older men as fathers, to younger men as brothers, to older women as mothers and to younger women as sisters (1 Tim. 5:1-2). Paul reminds Timothy that the headwaters of his faith are his mother and grandmother (2 Tim. 1:5).

Singleness and family life are not incompatible. In fact, they need to exist in the same hub to keep singleness from degenerating into something hurtful. Singles who have no extended family life are emotionally and spiritually vulnerable because they lack emotional support and spiritual covering. On the other hand, when singles are properly a part of a secure setting, either their own family or an adopted one, they are able to live a life of "undistracted devotion to the Lord."

Children As the Keys

If doing ministry as a couple is superb, it gets even better when children are incorporated into the staff. The devil wants us to perceive children as weak so that our energies and resources become absorbed in caring for them rather than enlisting them to help us "subdue the earth" (Gen. 1:28).

Psalm 127 deals with combining family, home and city reaching in a positive way. It opens by pointing to the need to build the home and secure the city. Then it moves on to admonish that "It is vain for [us] to rise up early, to retire late, to eat the bread of painful labors" (vv. 1,2). Why? Because all of that fretting will not help build the home or keep the city safe. The answer is something that "He gives to His beloved even in his sleep" (v. 2).

What is it that God gives that can accomplish what strenuous hyperactivity will not? Children! "Behold, children are a *gift* of the LORD; the fruit of the womb is a reward" (v. 3, emphasis mine). Please, do not miss the connection: God *gives,* and children are pictured as *gifts* from God.

God would not tell Adam and Eve to move on to multiply (children) in order to subdue the whole earth unless children are a plus instead of a minus. Nor would God imply in this psalm that children are meant to edify the home and guard the city if they are not. This is where we need to change paradigms. Children are a phenomenal addition that definitely tips the balance in our favor, "Like arrows in the hand of a warrior, so are the children of one's youth. How blessed is the man whose quiver is full of them" (vv. 4,5). This connection is the key.

A Threat to the Enemy

Children are arrows in the quiver that must be pulled out to face the enemy. This refers to children deployed in ministry. Psalm 127 pictures children as a threat to the enemy rather than a drain on resources or a focal point for parental worries.

The devil wants us to believe that our offspring are weak, vulnerable and incapable of fighting. If we buy into this lie we will spend the bulk of our time and energy protecting them. A soldier that fights *for* (to protect) rather than *with* the arrows in his quiver will soon be defeated.

The Devil Not Welcome

Notice how the psalm closes with a note of victory: "They shall not be ashamed, when they speak with their enemies in the gate"

(v. 5). There is a transition from singular to plural pronouns here, from "the man whose quiver is full of arrows" to "they [who] speak with their enemies in the gate." Who does "they" refer to? It refers to parents and their children standing together while facing their enemies. Where are the enemies? They are not inside the house, nor in the city, but in the gates. The gates of the city represent the outermost limit. That is where the devil belongs, away from our homes and out of our cities. The distance between the home and the gates is the range of an arrow fired by an expert archer. Children are designed to function in ministry, especially in spiritual warfare. It is about time to release them! Just look at what Jesus said when He prayed for children:

> Let the little children come to Me, and do not forbid them; for of such is the kingdom of God. Assuredly, I say to you, whoever does not receive the kingdom of God as a little child will by no means enter it (Luke 18:16,17, *NKJV*).

Coming Full Circle

To release children into ministry we need to see the image of God restored in men and women, since both genders have been entrusted with equal roles. Husbands and wives need to experience a powerful visitation of God for restoration to occur. Out of this awakening will come the empowering of children when God "will restore the hearts of the fathers to their children, and the hearts of the children to their fathers" so that the curse will be removed from our land (Mal. 4:6).

This is a tall order and one that requires overflowing grace. To learn more about this, in the next chapter we will go back to the abused lady whose story I began to tell in chapter five. Her story is a dramatic reflection of what is needed, and the final outcome is a living parable of the power that is in store for all of us.

Notes

1. Gary Greig provided the following insightful information: In this passage the Greek word "aner" (husband/man) should be translated as "husband," not as "man." Also, the Greek word "gune" (wife/woman) should be translated as "wife," not "woman" because of the parallelism of the language and themes in 1 Corinthians 11 and Ephesians 5:22,23, which clearly addresses husbands and wives.

2. In Genesis 2:18, the Greek *ezer kenegdo* means a "helper equal to him" or "helper corresponding completely to him." Francis Brown, et al, *The Brown-Driver-Briggs Hebrew and English Lexicon* (Peabody, MA: Hendrickson Publishers, 1996), p. 617.

CHAPTER TWELVE

THE ANSWER TO THE QUESTION WHY

The lady asked why, then stood there waiting for an answer. She wanted to know why she had been brutally hurt by her sexually abusive father. Why her personality had been fragmented. Why anger was still consuming her. Why the emotional baggage was still breaking her back even though she was now a Christian. Is not the gospel supposed to take care of all of that?

Those are fair questions because the gospel is good news, not just good advice. Good advice is what a banker gives when providing the address of the Salvation Army to someone he has just foreclosed on. Good news is when he tells the person that someone has just paid the overdue mortgage in full and has also left an extra million dollars!

Good News Instead of Good Advice

Too many Christians are tired of listening to good advice instead of good news. They have exhausted their ability to hope while trying to cope with problems that grow worse by the day. The Bible does not use the verb "to cope." Its biblical equivalent is "to overcome." God wants us to *overcome* our problems.

Finding answers to the questions posed by this lady is crucial to gender reconciliation. Even though women are usually the targets of abuse, men also get hurt. There is pain and misery on both sides of the fence. The fence must come down, hands have to be held and eyes have to turn to someone greater than all of us.

It is necessary to forgive sins and to cleanse the unrighteousness caused by them. For gender reconciliation to happen we need to learn how to forgive not once but millions of times. We must do this not for a day or a season but for a lifetime. The good news is that it is possible. The better news is that we can begin today.

Asking the Right Question

I sensed that the lady, whom I first mentioned in chapter five, had asked that question many times before and that she had been repeatedly disappointed by the lack of a satisfying answer. Now she stood waiting, expecting to be punished again by the familiar and deafening silence.

I told her that the question why is Satan's favorite. No one can answer it but God, because it requires knowledge of every factor and possibility. Instead I suggested a different question: What for?

By asking "What for?" she would be seeking what God wants to accomplish through the events of her life in the future, rather than what she had done wrong to deserve such treatment in the past. If she were to find a redeeming purpose behind her tragedy, the hopelessness that was destroying her would lift. Purpose turns pain into a servant instead of a master. It is not the same for a woman to have a severe toothache at 2 A.M. as it would be for her to go into labor in the middle of the night. Even though the latter causes more intense pain, she looks forward to an *increase* in the pain because of the *purpose* behind it: to give birth to a baby.

The woman at the conference I was speaking at asked how there could be any redemption in so much misery. I reminded her that 4 out of 10 women suffer some form of sexual abuse or molestation. If she were to find a solution, she would be able to help them. When other victims would look at her they would see two things: that she knew how they felt because of what she had gone through and that she had the solution because of the hope they would detect in her.

Where Was God?

"Where was God when I was being violated?" she demanded.

I told her that I did not know the answer, but since it was a fair question we should try to find out. Then I led her on an exercise designed to visit every year of her life beginning with her earliest memory.

We moved up one year at a time, revisiting her emotions until we got to the day when her mother had not believed her and she was on her way to the rushing river. I asked her, "Why didn't you throw yourself into the river?"

She claimed she did not know. I encouraged her to think about it. She said, "I can't."

I insisted and she cried, "I don't want to do it."

Gently but firmly I urged her to keep going. As she tried, her face began to twitch, her body shook, and an abundance of tears flowed. I could see she was desperately trying to break through a wall of repressed emotions held together by pain and bitterness. This went on for a while; then just when I was becoming concerned that she might not be able to endure any more, she burst into a radiant smile.

Opening her eyes with obvious delight she exclaimed, "I see Him, I see Him!"

I asked whom she was seeing. She said, "Jesus. He was there by the river. He embraced me and comforted me. That is why I did not jump into it."

We kept advancing one year at a time until we got to the moment when she tried to slash her veins. The same scenario of initial pain developed to be eventually replaced by great joy. This time she said, "I see it. I see it. An angel came and covered me with his wings."

I told her that since God has been so close to her there was reason to believe that the ultimate outcome was going to be positive.

Multiple Personalities

"Are you positive?" she asked. "What about my multiple personalities? You have no idea what a terrible existence I live. I have never felt whole as a person, and I never know when the violent one might take over."

I explained to her that the fragmentation of her personality is what had kept her from going insane, since it is impossible for a child to keep in the same picture the father she instinctively loves and the beast who rapes her. Fragmentation of the psyche had allowed her to turn off, and thus protect, some pieces of the picture during the violent acts. I assured her that God could and would heal her.

I had seen something similar before and knew for a fact that God could heal such a condition. My wife, Ruth, and I had ministered to a student at Moody Bible Institute who came to us in total distress. This student was at the end of her emotional rope. She had been through every form of counseling imaginable trying to deal with the 11 fragments into which her personality had broken. While she talked I had asked God what I should do, and I clearly sensed Him saying: "Assure her that I will heal her. Then pray a prayer of faith." Ruth and I did exactly as God had instructed, and the next day the young woman was totally transformed.

She told us that during the night she went through intense pain in her soul, as if bones that had not been properly set were being broken and then reset. When she woke up she felt whole for the first time in her life. We checked on her three months later, and she was doing even better. We knew that God was able to heal this terrible condition.

No More BB Guns

The woman at the conference next asked about her out-of-control anger. She shared how much she regretted that her father had died before she could kill him. Her anger was so intense that she assured me that if her father were in the room she would murder him without any remorse. "What about my anger?" she cried.

"Sister," I said, "that anger is what kept you from total despair since it provided you with hope—a very imperfect and evil one, but hope nonetheless. But it failed to help you. It was like giving you a BB gun to shoot at a charging rhino. You need a bigger weapon. I want to put in your hands a bazooka loaded for bear for you to fire at close range."

I finally got her attention. She asked, "What is that?"

I explained that she had received the grace of God in vain, something Paul warned the Corinthians not to do (see 2 Cor. 6:1).

Gone in 30 Minutes

What I shared next changed her life forever. In fewer than 30 minutes, half a century of dark misery was turned into a shining trophy of God's grace. This is the message that is needed to bridge the gender gap and to wash away the oozing filth of sin and anger that is defiling people all over the world. It is the message of how not to receive the grace of God in vain.

What do I mean?

The devil cannot stop God from bestowing grace upon us, because God is all mighty.

The devil cannot stop God from bestowing grace upon us, because God is all mighty. Neither can he prevent us from receiving it, because God always finishes what He starts. Since Satan cannot prevent grace from reaching us, he focuses on preventing us from *applying* it to the sin for which it is intended.

He has been most effective when it comes to our hurts. Hurts are the tangible dimensions of sins committed against us. The only way to deal with sin is through grace, and this is why God gives us grace to treat the sin hurting us. However, the evil one tells us that such grace is no good unless the offender repents and asks for our forgiveness. He wants us to believe that grace has to be activated through the repentance of the one who offended us.

This is a grim proposition, because if the offender does not cooperate we are put in a very vulnerable position: hurt once, we continue to be hurt by the offender's refusal to repent.

However, a lack of repentance on the part of the violator is not an obstacle that keeps grace from being extended. When someone sins against us, God automatically gives us grace to deal with it. Being sinned against provides us with the jurisdiction necessary to forgive. God forgives on the vertical dimension but only the injured party can forgive a personal offense on the horizontal level.

When Jesus died on the cross, He shed His blood for the sins of the world and everybody was forgiven. However, how many people around the Cross actually experienced forgiveness? One did for sure: the thief hanging next to Jesus. Perhaps two did if we count the Centurion. Even though only a couple received forgiveness, everybody was forgiven. This was so because grace is activated by the one sinned against (Christ), not by the one who sinned.

The Power of Grace

It is always the option of the injured party to forgive. Satan knows this and he works hard to convince us that there is nothing we can do until the offender repents.

Believing this lie causes us to receive the grace of God in vain. It is like a person dying of pneumonia who receives the right antibiotics, puts them on the night table, but never takes them—a few days later, he dies. Even though he *receives* the medication, he fails to *take* it. This is what Paul is writing about in 2 Corinthians 6:1: "We also urge you not to receive the grace of God in vain." It is not enough to receive it. It has to be applied to sin.

The most painful hurts are inflicted by people we cannot erase from our lives, such as relatives, associates and partners. Furthermore, no matter how old the hurt, it's as if it is repeated every day because of the constant-replay mechanism built into the hurt.

Counting the Hurts

Have you ever been hurt? I am sure you can give me an all-points bulletin on more than one offender. You know the transgressions very well. You remember every detail. Since these hurts are so fresh in your mind, I wonder if they happened today, perhaps this morning? No, you say. They happened a long time ago, but continue to happen every day as you remember them. If you are like everyone else, you probably add new layers of pain to the initial ones.

Once I counseled a very elderly man who was so old that he had wrinkles inside his wrinkles. In whispers and through clenched teeth he told me a pitiful story of pain and abuse. As he did, tears began to roll down the maze of wrinkles on his cheeks. As I watched them I told myself, "Those tears must be the most bitter tears in the world, since this man is in so much pain."

When he was done telling me about an offense, I asked him, "Roger, how long ago was this?" He looked at me through the smeared glass of hopelessness and shame clouding his eyes and said, "Fifty years." Even though it happened half a century ago, it was happening again right before our eyes.

Roger had heard countless sermons on grace and forgiveness. He had been prayed for more times than he cared to remember, but not much had changed. Why? Because even though he received plenty of grace, he received it in vain. His nightstand was stacked with bottles of the right medicine, but he never took it because he had been waiting for the offender to dispense it to him. What a waste of grace!

Letting Go of the Offense

To see how applying grace works, let us first look at the Scriptures: "If anyone is in Christ, he is a new creation; old things have passed away; behold, all things have become new" (2 Cor. 5:17, *NKJV*).

At what point in your life did the new things of God begin to take hold? If you answered "At the moment of conversion," you may have received the grace of God in vain. You may now find yourself holding two baskets. One would contain the new things Jesus has been giving you since your conversion. You want everybody to see this basket. But in the other hand you are holding a second basket, and you are protectively hiding it behind your back. You do not want anyone to see what is in this basket because it contains the old things that happened prior to your conversion.

If this is your situation then you may also find yourself saying, "I wish I had known Jesus sooner. I am grateful for the salvation and the many new things He has given me. However, some of the old things I did before coming to Jesus have scarred me, and now I live in their shadow."

This does not sound like good news. In fact, it is terrible news. This is the equivalent of spiritual schizophrenia, and it represents the opposite of what God wants for your life.

What actually happens at the moment of conversion is that the grace of God enters our life and goes all the way back to the moment of conception, turning every old thing into a new one. This is possible because God makes all things work together for good.

He takes what the devil intended for evil and uses it for good. Where sin abounds He makes grace overflow. Sin can never outflow grace; it is always the other way around. This is illustrated by Paul's testimony. Before his conversion the ugliest *old thing* in his life was that he was the *destroyer* of the faith. After his conversion he became the *builder* of the Church.

The Totality of Life

The landscape of our soul was scarred with all kinds of evil deeds. God's grace at the moment of conversion is intended to transform our old lives. He did not save just that part of our lives that began the day we were born again. He saved the totality of our life, from the moment of conception on. This is the way it ought to be, because if there is an area in our lives that needs transformation it is the one before accepting Christ as Savior.

Because conception is when life begins it is also when *old things* can start to happen. As a minister, I often see evidence of this in counseling. There are people who struggle with terrible rejection and do not know why. After asking a battery of questions, the source of the problem remains elusive. However, when I ask such a person, "Are you the result of an unwanted pregnancy?" an immediate hit is registered.

Why?

Because when the mother found out that she was a few weeks pregnant she became upset and wished the pregnancy would go away, thus unwillingly and unknowingly introducing the first old thing. A person with such a background may become a Christian at age 5 or age 50, but unless the grace of God reaches all the way to the moment of conception to turn that first old thing into a new one, he will live in misery. He will make it to heaven but in the meantime will live in hell on Earth.

The Benefits of Grace

Grace is intended to deal with every sin in our lives, not just those committed *by* us but also those committed *against* us. God's design is for His grace to travel the length of our lives, touch every evil deed and then set us, and those who have hurt us, free from the curse of sin.

Why is it so difficult to comprehend that the same grace that erases our sin also cancels the sins others have committed against us? It is difficult because, as Westerners, we take an individualistic approach to life. We have been taught to believe that God deals with us as individuals. Even though this is correct, it is also true that God deals with us corporately. In the Bible there are plenty of examples when the sin, or the repentance of one person, cursed or blessed groups of people (see Jos. 7:1-26; Ezra 9:5-15; 10:1). We tend to browse quickly over those passages because we, as Westerners, find them difficult, but they are found throughout the Scriptures.

Sin, even *personal* sin, is corporate in its consequences, and needs to be dealt with corporately as well. If a husband commits adultery, the innocent wife will be affected as well as his children, his ministry and his church. There is no way around this corporate dimension of sin. Therefore, if grace is God's remedy for sin, to deal effectively with it, grace has to be corporate in its benefits also. This is tremendous good news.

If a sinner repents, God will forgive him or her immediately, thus cutting off the flow of defilement created by his sin. But if he or she does not repent, God makes grace available to those affected in order to contain, and even reverse, the degradation caused by sin.

Through the Eyes of Christ

Before we can reach the point of receiving the grace Christ offers to each of us, we need to see the one who sinned against us as God sees him or her this side of Calvary. The key is found in 2 Corinthians 5:16: "From now on we recognize no man according to the flesh; even though we have known Christ according to the flesh, yet now we know Him thus no longer."

We have a choice: We can see the offender in Christ or in the flesh. In the flesh his or her sin is still active and deserves punishment, but in Christ it is already forgiven, even though he or she has not claimed the benefit. It was dealt with by Jesus' blood. If and when that person repents, Christ will not shed His blood again to deal with it, since He already did so once and forever.

The Dad, the Daughter and the Bee

This principle of God's grace presents us with the option to see the offender either in the fleshly (natural) unforgiven state or as already forgiven in Christ. Paul exhorts us to see him *in Christ* and to treat him accordingly. This is illustrated by the story of the dad, the daughter and the bee.

A man was driving his car on the freeway on a hot summer day. The windows were up, the car air conditioning was on, and his five-year-old daughter was seated next to him. All of a sudden she began to scream, "Daddy, there is a bee inside the car. It is going to sting me. I am afraid, Daddy. Please, do something!"

The dad tried to keep one eye on the road while he searched for the bee with the other. He finally caught the bee and held it tightly in his hand until it stung him. Next, taking the bee by its wings, he showed it to his daughter, who panicked even more. She cried, "Daddy, it is going to sting me. It is going to sting me." Pointing to the wound on the palm of his hand he said, "Don't be afraid. It can't hurt you because it already stung me." This is exactly what Christ did on the cross. The sin committed against us was dealt with by the stripes He suffered. He paid the price so that abundant grace can be available to us to deal with it from a horizontal perspective.

Why So Much Pain?

You may say, "If my sin is already dealt with, why does it hurt so much?" Because the wages of sin is death (see Rom. 6:23). Therefore, unremitted sins remain active, generating death, day after day. If a person was beaten or raped a long time ago, the physical dimension no longer hurts. The bruises and the pain are long gone. What still hurts is the death that the unremitted sin keeps generating. Sin is still active, and it will remain so until Jesus' blood is applied to it. To do this the sinner must be seen *in Christ* and his sin as forgiven.

Tougher Than Nails

Somehow the devil wants us to believe that grace is soft like jelly. On the contrary, grace is tougher than nails. Applying grace to undeserving sins is not an act of weakness but of great spiritual courage. Grace was Jesus' weapon of choice while He hung naked, abandoned by His disciples, forsaken by His father and surrounded by demons. He looked weak and vulnerable, without anything to fight back with except grace.

He reached for it, and in a moment He turned everything around. Satan was disarmed and paraded in defeat (see Col. 2:14-16). The thief believed in Jesus. The Centurion acknowledged His divinity. The multitudes went away beating their breasts and convinced that they had made a mistake by consenting to His execution. The Father was able to open a way for sinners to flee Satan's dungeons. In one second the sins of the entire world were atoned for. All of that because Jesus chose grace rather than judgment.

Grace changes the worst sin into the best trophy. This is the same grace that Paul warns us not to receive in vain.

Turning Curses into Blessings

Grace is so powerful that it can turn the worst situation into the best. The most evil sin ever committed on planet Earth was the crucifixion of Jesus. It happened on a cross. However, today the cross is a symbol of blessing. Believers wear them around their necks. Crosses are stamped on Bible covers, erected on top of buildings, sung about with deep emotion and gratitude. Very few things elicit more joy than the Cross.

> # The greater the sin committed against you, the greater the grace God has *already* made available to you.

However, before Jesus' death it was a symbol of cursing: "Cursed is everyone who hangs on a tree" (Gal. 3:13). When did it change from a curse to a blessing? At the moment Jesus wrapped grace around it. When He cried out, "Father, forgive them; for they do not know what they are doing" (Luke 23:34). He turned the curse of the Cross into the blessing we know today. Grace did it.

Let the Holy Spirit speak to you right now. Let Him assure you that the greater the sin committed against you, the greater the grace God has *already* made available to you. You can turn those curses into blessings just as Jesus did.

A Dying Example of Living Faith

You may say that intellectually you understand how Jesus did it, but that you feel you cannot respond in the same manner because you are just a human being. If this is what you are feeling, let me point to the case of Stephen in Acts 7, since he was a human being, just like you and me. He was preaching to a most unreceptive crowd. Even though his face looked like that of an angel, his audience grew angrier by the minute until they turned into a mob and charged against him. They pushed him over the edge of a cliff and began to stone him. Saul of Tarsus, who would later become Paul, was one of the leaders of the angry mob.

As those stones, thrown in anger, hit Stephen they cracked his skull and broke his ribs—Stephen began to drown in his own blood! Every time he looked up he saw angry faces; Saul's was the angriest one. But beyond that raging crowd he also saw the heavens open and Jesus standing up. Strangely, Jesus was not seated at the right hand of the Father, interceding. Instead, He stood in a posture of judgment. Some theologians have suggested that He did this because Israel was close to committing the unforgivable sin.

What did Stephen do in such a context of sin and judgment? Seeing so much sin, he asked the Father for extraordinary grace. He cried out, "Lord, do not hold this sin against them" (see Acts 7:60).

Turning Saul into Paul

The Father obliged Stephen and two chapters later Saul of Tarsus, the destroyer, became Paul, the builder of the Church (see Acts 9). As Paul lay on the side of the road to Damascus there was no need for anyone to lead him to Christ. Stephen deserves the credit. It all began when he applied grace to the sin

Paul had committed against him. Saul did not ask for grace, but Stephen extended it to him anyway with extraordinary results. Grace is indeed powerful!

This is the same grace available to you today. Angry people are stoning you with mean words and evil deeds that feel like rocks. Like Stephen, you are in pain. But you also can choose to see the offender *in Christ* rather than in the natural. His or her sin against you already stung Jesus. There is no need for it to sting you any longer if you apply grace to it.

You may say, "Stephen was a servant of God, filled with the Holy Spirit and doing God's work, but I am just a struggling believer." In that case, let me ask you, "What about the lady who was victimized by incest?" I doubt there are many people who have suffered as much. Let me tell you how she found freedom by applying grace rather than just receiving it.

Now or Never

After I explained these truths, that lady asked, "Are you saying that I must forgive my father, apply grace to the pile of hideous sins he committed against me?" When I replied in the affirmative she lost control and began to scream, "Never! Never! I hate him. One of my greatest regrets is that he died before I could kill him myself."

I told her in a gentle but firm way, "You have lived 55 years in hell. If you live twice as long it is bound to get worse each year. Your only option is to apply grace. You do not have to feel like it. Just do it."

At that moment the Holy Spirit overpowered her and she agreed to do it. Through clenched teeth she forgave her father and blessed his memory. Next, I laid hands on her head and prayed that God would heal her psyche, reuniting the broken fragments of her personality.

Whole at Last

The next day I moved on to another assignment. Occasionally I remembered her, but it was not until almost a year later that I came back to her town to preach in a stadium event. While I was in the hospitality room, next to the platform, the door opened and a woman walked in. When I looked up I recognized the lady for whom I had prayed. She shook my hand enthusiastically. I asked how she was doing. She replied, "I am struggling. I struggle every day, every minute and sometimes every second. But there is a difference between struggling and always losing and struggling and always winning. And I am winning. Hatred no longer controls me."

I inquired about her fragmented personality. She smiled generously and said, "I am whole. For the first time in my life I am no longer fragmented. God healed me!"

What an extraordinary miracle! Grace is indeed tougher than nails. It is definitely more powerful than sin; and it should be, since it is God's remedy for sin.

Satan's Nemesis

In the past all the devil had to do to torture this lady was to whisper the word "incest." The moment he did, she would collapse. Now she stands up in front of victims of incest, and, by proclaiming *grace*, she tortures the same demons that used to torment her. By bringing hope to others with whom she shares so much in common she has found a redemptive purpose for her traumatic childhood. God is using for good that which the devil intended for evil.

Your Turn

What about you? What about those hurts that are constantly replaying in your mind, day after day, month after month? You will not be able to forgive others until you allow the grace of God to flow all the way back to touch every evil thing done *by* you and *to* you. You must exchange the *old things* for *new things*. That this is possible is encouraging. That it can happen right now is most exhilarating.

Learning to forgive is essential for reconciliation since no one can give what he or she does not have. We need to experience grace at the deepest level and then be *eager* to pass it on to others in our circles of relationships.

For men and women to be restored they need to apply grace to each other day after day. For marriages to be rebuilt grace needs to flow between the spouses. The upcoming rematch will feature the Lord of grace against the lord of sin. God has chosen to disguise His troops as doves. Doves are peaceful birds. The Holy Spirit, who is the minister of grace, was likewise represented by a dove at Jesus' baptism. Grace was the key then, and it still is the key now.

Wherever you are reading these words, I urge you to *choose* to apply grace to every person that has hurt you right now. Take every sin committed against you by members of the opposite sex, by leaders, by peers and by relatives, put them in a pile and cover them with the grace that God has *already* given you, which is part of the grace that first saved you. Of course, if you have never accepted Christ as Savior, you need to do that first. But if you are a believer, you do not have to ask for additional grace. It is already in you. The Lord's prayer says it very clearly: "[Father] forgive us our sins, for we also forgive everyone who sins against us" (Luke 11:4, *NIV*). It is all part of the same deposit.

Just let it travel the length of your soul all the way back to your earliest memory and watch it turn old things into new things. This is what grace does best, it turns sin into blessings. The bigger the sin, the greater the trophy it is able to produce.

I urge you to pray this prayer right now:

> *Father God, I thank You for the grace that Jesus bestowed*
> *on me when He died. I also thank You that such grace was*
> *intended not just for me but for everybody else. It forgave*
> *my sins as well as their sins.*
> *Please allow that grace to touch every person who has touched*
> *me with evil intent and everyone who has sinned against me.*
> *Let it be known in heaven and on Earth that as of this moment*
> *they are forgiven by the same grace that I was forgiven by.*
> *Father, I also pray that You bless them. I ask You to restore and*
> *to prosper them. I pray for them every blessing I have ever*
> *prayed for myself. I set them free, and in so doing*
> *I set myself free by the same grace.*
> *In the name of Jesus our Lord I pray.*

CHAPTER THIRTEEN

WOMEN'S FINEST HOUR

Early in the morning, after having spent the night at His favorite prayer mountain, the Mount of Olives, Jesus went to the Temple. When all the people came to Him, He sat down and began to teach (see John 8:1,2). It was a peaceful setting that Jesus definitely enjoyed.

Suddenly, the tranquillity was rudely shattered when the scribes and Pharisees forcibly brought before Him a woman caught in adultery. They demanded that Jesus sanction her death as prescribed by the Law. At first, Jesus did not answer. He just stooped down and, with his finger, wrote on the ground, while the religious leaders persisted in their demands for lethal force (see John 8:3-6).

As terrible as the sin of this woman was, she should not have had to stand accused alone, since it takes two people to commit adultery. Where was the man? Why was he not also brought in? The Law specifies that both of them should be stoned. In the eyes of the accusers it was all right to condemn the woman but not the man. What a contradiction!

Equal Responsibility

The picture above is similar to what we often see in ministry circles today. People driven by excessive zeal intentionally focus on passages of the Scriptures that favor their biased points of view. They demand judgment on women "caught . . . in the very act" (John 8:4) without paying attention to men's share of responsibility for the violation. While this goes on, women stand exposed, humiliated and defiled. Deprived of legitimate male covering, they are often driven to adulterous substitutes.

While Jesus wrote on the ground, He chose not to bring up men's sins in general and not to ask that the male adulterer also be brought in. Neither did He tell the self-righteous accusers that they were as guilty as the woman and the man caught in adultery. He, however, knew this was true, because He was able to read the men's hearts.

Why did He keep quiet? Because He is a reconciler, not a divider. He is an intercessor, not an accuser. He purposely refused to take sides because taking sides is what the devil does. Jesus came "to seek and to save that which was lost" (Luke 19:10). And what was lost is not in one piece or in one pile. It is broken and scattered all over the place. He does not pick the best-looking parts and reject the most damaged ones. He waits until He is able to embrace all the broken pieces, take them in His arms, place them close to His heart and then fix them!

In the same manner, Jesus refuses to take sides when it comes to the gender gap. He will not lower men in order to elevate women or vice versa. Instead, He meets them at whatever level they are at in order to bring *both* of them up to His level. This is the way of the Cross. Jesus is faithful, even when we are unfaithful, because He cannot deny Himself. He is a Savior, not a condemner.

A Radical Message

Is Jesus' approach effective? Yes! Where do you think those men went after they left Jesus that day? Most likely they went home to their wives. Having seen themselves reflected on the troubled face of the accused woman, they must have realized how close they had come, at one time or another, to standing accused like her. Jesus' silence forever stamped the ugliness of adultery in their memory.

To the woman He said, "From now on sin no more" (John 8:11). What a liberating message overflowing with so much hope! Rather than dwelling on the past, He covered it with mercy and pointed the woman in the direction of restorative holiness. Sinning no more meant breaking up with her fellow adulterer and repairing her damaged marriage—a difficult but necessary assignment that calls for gender reconciliation at the deepest level.

Is such a radical change possible? Yes! Immediately after uttering the command not to sin anymore, Jesus proclaimed, "I am the light of the world; he who follows Me shall not walk in darkness, but shall have the light of life" (John 8:12). He knows about our darkness. He knows we need His light. Rather than cursing our darkness, He shines for us to see the way and to follow Him. When we do, we leave darkness behind, forever.

Shortly after Jesus declared He was the light of the world, a very intense theological discussion erupted. At first, many people resisted His words and accused Him of false testimony, a severe offense under the law. However, Jesus stood firm. He said, "When you lift up the Son of Man, then you will know that I am He" (John 8:28). When the crowd heard His unwavering words, "many came to believe in Him" (John 8:30).

What does it mean that those who "lift up the Son of Man . . . will know that I am He?" The word "man" in "Son of Man" does not refer only to males. It is the Greek word *anthropos*, which includes both men and women.

It is about time we lift up the Son of Man, the Savior of both men and women. When we see Jesus as the Son of Man (anthropos), we will find that in Him, men and women are reconciled; we will take our position in Christ, and we will begin to minister harmoniously side by side, like Adam and Eve did in the Garden.

A Victory Parade

This is what Psalm 68 intimates. Following the surprise victory where women played a decisive role, the Lord led a triumphant parade: "The chariots of God are myriads, thousands upon thousands; The Lord is among them as at Sinai, in holiness" (Ps. 68:17).

In biblical days it was customary for victorious kings to give some of the best captives as gifts to people under their jurisdiction. This is precisely what God did here: "Thou hast ascended on high, thou hast led captivity captive, thou hast received gifts for men" (Ps. 68:18, *KJV*).

Equipping All the Saints

This particular passage is referred to by Paul in Ephesians 4:8,11:

> When He ascended on high, He led captive a host of cap-
> tives, and He gave gifts to men. And He gave some as
> apostles, and some as prophets, and some as evangelists,
> and some as pastors and teachers.

This is the section from which we have developed the doctrine of
the governmental offices in the Church: apostles, prophets,
evangelists, pastors and teachers.

At first it may seem contradictory that such a defining passage be linked to a psalm that highlights the role of women,
because those offices are traditionally held by men. But the link
is very appropriate when we understand that those offices are
designed to develop the *entire* Church into a state that reflects
integration and harmony between both genders, "for the equipping of [all] the saints for the work of service, to the building up
of the [entire] body of Christ" (Eph. 4:12).

This is how Paul describes the outcome of such equipping:

> Until we *all* attain to the unity of the faith, and of the
> knowledge of the Son of God, to a mature man, to the
> measure of the stature which belongs to the *fulness* of
> Christ . . . from whom the *whole* body, being fitted and
> held together by that which *every* joint supplies, accord-
> ing to the proper working of *each individual* part, causes
> the growth of the body for the building up of itself in
> love (Eph. 4:13-16, emphasis mine).

The abundance of superlatives—"all," "fulness," "whole" and
"every"—is indicative of an ideal that will be reached through a

process as indicated by the expression "*until* we all attain . . . the fulness of Christ" (v. 13, emphasis mine).

When we put this passage in the context of its source, Psalm 68, we find reason to conclude that God's triumphant parade expresses the full restoration of the genders described in Joel's prophecy (see chapter eight) and alluded to by Paul in Ephesians.

This fits perfectly with the reference in Joel's prophecy to sons and daughters, bondservants and maidservants ministering side by side under the power and the presence of the Holy Spirit (see Acts 2:16-18). Whether in a loving, affirming setting such as the family (sons and daughters) or in a demeaning, debasing social inequity (bondservants and maidservants), when filled with the Spirit of God, men and women will stand and minister together. And when they do so, signs and wonders will take place, the world will be shaken "and it shall be, that everyone who calls on the name of the LORD shall be saved" (Acts 2:21).

The greatest harvest in history shall be brought in by men and women working side by side, and Jesus' enemies will become a footstool for Him.

The Heart of Hope

At that precise moment, the greatest harvest in the history of the Church shall be brought in by men and women working side by side, and Jesus' enemies will become a footstool for Him (see Acts 2:35). All of this will happen in the intimacy of family-centered ministry as implied by the reference to young men and old men (children and parents) and daughters and sons (see Acts 2:17).

This is the heart of the hope before us. God does not expect that we fix the world so that men and women can be reconciled. He asks the opposite: men and women who have been captured by Him should stand together in His presence, filled with His Spirit, because the extraordinary ministry that will emanate from such a united stance will change the world. Reconciliation is not the result of ministry but the premier precondition for it. None of this will happen until men and women of all ages, whether married, single or widowed, have been overpowered by the Spirit of God as on the Day of Pentecost.

The devil knows this and he will do everything permissible to him to stop such a reconciliation. He knows that if all men and women stand together in ministry, "God will shatter the head of His enemies . . . [and their] foot [will] shatter them in blood" (Ps. 68: 21-23).

God's Strategy

The reference to the foot doing the crushing provides a possible answer to one of the most often asked questions among Christians: Why not headship for women? The answer is a very edifying one.

Women's positioning is not intended to demean them but is part of God's strategy. God allows women to be camouflaged as flocks of silvery doves, resting on stained sheepfolds, hiding in lowly places while He waits for His enemies to exalt themselves. However, when He finally deploys women, everyone will see the gold—until then hidden—glistening on their pinions and will come to appreciate their value. No one will see it more clearly than the men standing next to them in ministry. In that hour, women's finest, everyone will see that they are indeed twice refined!

Additional Works by Ed Silvoso

THAT NONE SHOULD PERISH VIDEO SEMINAR
This breakthrough video series is the live version of Ed Silvoso's best-selling book, *That None Should Perish*. Each of the sixteen lessons are broken into 35 minute segments, which makes it perfect for Bible studies, Sunday School classes, or pastors prayer groups. Includes reproducible syllabus. (Four 2-hour videotapes)

LIGHT THE NATION ONE HOUSE AT A TIME Starter Kit
This starter kit by Ed Silvoso includes a 7-minute motivational video, 30-minute how-to audio cassette on Lighthouses of Prayer and a Lighthouse Guidebook. This is an excellent motivational and training tool for both individuals and groups. (Video tape, audio tape, guidebook)

VICTORY AT HOME!
This four tape audio series is a timely message that will help parents prepare their children for a successful marriage, as well as evaluate the condition of their own marriage relationship. Singles will also find this series encouraging as they trust God for their life partner. (Four 60-minute audio tapes)

BECOMING AN OVERCOMER
This two tape series will help you to not only pull down the strongholds that have kept you from living a victorious Christian life, but will also allow you to see how God can turn the worst tragedy in your life into a trophy of His love when grace is applied to those who have hurt you. Two life-changing topics! (Two 60-minute audio tapes)

Acquire these and other titles through Harvest Evangelism's on-line book-store at www.harvestevan.org, *or by contacting them at:*

Harvest Evangelism, Inc.
P.O. Box 20310 • San Jose, CA 95160-0310
Tel (800)835-7979 • (408)350-1669 • Fax (408)927-9830

Experience Prayer Evangelism first-hand with Ed Silvoso by participating in one of Harvest Evangelism's Argentina training trips (Summer and Fall).
Call (408)927-9052 today.

Inspiring Reading
for Women

Moments Together for Couples
Daily Devotions for Drawing Near
to God and One Another
Dennis and Barbara Rainey
Hardcover
ISBN 08307.17544

Where Hearts Are Shared
Simple Recipies for Entertaining from
Women Around the World
Jane Hansen
Hardcover
ISBN 08307.28937

Beauty Restored
Finding Life and Hope After
Date Rape
Me Ra Koh
Trade Paper
ISBN 08307.27612

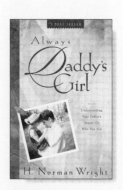

Always Daddy's Girl
Understanding Your Father's
Impact on Who You Are
H. Norman Wright
Trade Paper
ISBN 08307.27620

Women of Destiny
Releasing You to Fulfill God's Call
in Your Life and in the Church
Cindy Jacobs
Trade Paper
ISBN 08307.18648

First Place
Lose Weight and
Keep It Off Forever
*Carole Lewis with
Terry Whalin*
Hard Cover
ISBN 08307.28635

Know Christ and Make Him Known

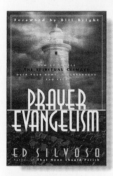

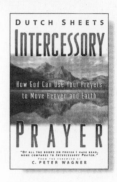

Prayer Evangelism
How to Change the Spiritual Climate over Your Home, Neighborhood and City
Ed Silvoso
Paperback
ISBN 08307.23978

That None Should Perish
How To Reach Entire Cities for Christ Through Prayer Evangelism
Ed Silvoso
Trade Paper
ISBN 08307.16904

Intercessory Prayer
How God Can Use Your Prayers to Move Heaven and Earth
Dutch Sheets
Trade Paper
ISBN 08307.19008

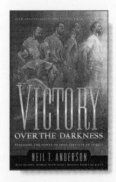

Beyond the Veil
Entering into Intimacy with God Through Prayer
Alice Smith
Trade Paper
ISBN 08307.20707

Living the Spirit-Formed Life
Growing in the 10 Principles of Spirit-Filled Discipleship
Jack Hayford
Trade Paper
ISBN 08307.27671

Victory over the Darkness
Realizing the Power of Your Identity in Christ
Neil T. Anderson
Trade Paper
ISBN 08307.25644